THE
NEO-GENERALIST

WHERE YOU GO IS WHO YOU ARE

Kenneth
Mikkelsen
&
Richard
Martin

Published by
LID Publishing
An imprint of LID Business Media Ltd.
LABS House, 15-19 Bloomsbury Way,
London, WC1A 2TH, UK

info@lidpublishing.com
www.lidpublishing.com

A member of:

BPR

businesspublishersroundtable.com

© Kenneth Mikkelsen & Richard Martin, 2019
© LID Publishing Limited, 2019
First edition published in 2016
Reprinted in 2021, 2023

Printed by Severn, Gloucester
ISBN: 978-1-912555-39-0

Cover and page design: Caroline Li

THE
NEO-GENERALIST

WHERE YOU GO IS WHO YOU ARE

MADRID | MEXICO CITY | LONDON
BUENOS AIRES | BOGOTA | SHANGHAI

FOR KRISTIAN, ILSE AND LOUISE

You are my Northern Stars
helping me to learn, love and live
and see the connection.

FOR BEN, IMI AND GABE

You changed my world.
Never lose your sense of wonder;
Stay curious and always question.

CONTENTS

*Wanderer, there is no road,
the road is made by walking.*

Antonio Machado, Campos de Castilla

PREFACE

We are multidimensional creatures and search for answers in many, complementary ways. Each serves a purpose, and we need them all.

Marcelo Gleiser, *The Island of Knowledge*

The neo-generalist is *both* specialist *and* generalist, often able to master multiple disciplines. We all carry within us the potential to specialise and generalise. Many of us are unwittingly eclectic, innately curious. There is a continuum between the extremes of specialism and generalism, a spectrum of possibilities. Where we stand on that continuum at a given point in time is governed by context.

Since the advent of the Industrial Revolution, our society has remained in thrall to the notion of hyperspecialism. This places constraints on the ways in which we are educated, the work we do, the people we socialise with, how we are recruited, how our career progression is managed, how we label ourselves for the benefit of others' understanding. To counter and challenge these social norms, the neo-generalist has to learn how to give expression to their more generalist tendencies, even as they practise various specialisms, guiding others as they do so.

Our workplaces, governments, intelligence agencies and other communities and institutions constantly complain of silos, but that is an inevitable consequence of our promotion of hyperspecialism. So too the myopia of expertise that prevents us from seeing properly what is right in front of us, or connecting it in meaningful ways with other information, other people.

In the following pages, we explore the characteristics and behaviours of individuals who do give space to their generalist inclinations, highlighting the social and organisational benefits that can be derived as a result of this. We ask how can the neo-generalist help shape our world, supporting and enabling others, as the current century progresses? To illustrate our idea, we draw on stories from multiple disciplines and cultures, from business, art, science and sport, from people who live in more than one world.

CAST

*There is no house
like the house of belonging.*

David Whyte, *The House of Belonging*

THE AUTHORS

Kenneth Mikkelsen – @KenHMikkelsen
Richard Martin – richardmartinwriter.com

Many people generously shared their time and ideas with us while we researched this book. We are indebted to them. The diversity of where they come from and what they do renders these people uniquely difficult to label. It is a trait shared by neo-generalists everywhere: the shunning of neat categorisation.

While we illuminate fragments of their stories throughout the book, there is so much more to say about each and every one of them. Many are active on social media. Several have written their own books, blog regularly and have been recorded speaking at public events. We encourage you to learn more about them and their work. These are people who embody what it is to be both interested and interesting.

THE INTERVIEWEES

Adina Forsström – @AdinaForsstrom
Al Smith – @_al_smith
Anand Mahindra – @anandmahindra
Anne McCrossan – @Annemcx
Bill Liao – @liaonet
Briony Marshall – @ArtBriony
Carl Gombrich – @carlgomb
Charles Handy – @charleshandy25
David Hain – @davidhain
Dolly Garland – @DollyGarland
Ed Brenegar – @edbrenegar
Eddie Harran – @eddieharran
Elizabeth Handy
Ella Saltmarshe – @saltsea
Erika Ilves – @erikailves
Geoffrey West
Grace Clapham – @agent_grace
Hans-Jürgen Sturm – @hjsturm
Henry Doss – @HenryHartDoss
Imandeep Kaur – @ImmyKaur
Indy Johar – @indy_johar
James Tyer – @jimbobtyer
Jane McConnell – @netjmc
John Michel
Jon Foster-Pedley – @JFPHenley
Jonas De Cooman – @JonasDeCooman
Jonathan Michie – @jonathan_michie
Kare Anderson – @KareAnderson
Lars Wetterberg
Lucas Amungwa
Lucian Tarnowski – @LucianT
Maggie MacDonald – @MacDonaldMaggie

Maria Moraes Robinson – @DoraMoraesR
Mark Storm – @marksstorm
Marvin Abrinica – @marvinador
Nada Taha Borisly – @Borisly
Nick Hixson – @Hixsons
Ole Fogh Kirkeby
Peter Bull
Peter Vander Auwera – @petervan
Prasad Kaipa – @PKaipa
Robin Chase – @rmchase
Rotana Ty – @rotanarotana
Sarah Miller Caldicott
Scott Torrance
Simon Terry – @simongterry
Solonia Teodros
Susy Paisley-Day – @SusyPaisley
Tamar Many
Tara Swart – @TaraSwart
Ting Kelly – @tingkelly

Once introduced, interviewees will frequently be referenced by their first names. This will distinguish them from other people whose work, ideas and achievements we have relied on during our research, including historical figures, philosophers, writers, artists, scientists, sports people and filmmakers.

PART

I.
GENERALISE
TO SPECIALISE

I am large, I contain multitudes.

Walt Whitman, *Song of Myself*

To wander the corridors of a hospital is to experience a sensory overload. The smells of cleaning products, institutional food, bad coffee, human decay and illness swirl in the air. Voices, both raised and murmured, compete with crashing doors and the alarms, beeps and susurrations of machines. Everywhere, too, there are graphics and signs demanding the attention of your eyes. This is a domain that has been fragmented and labelled; the cartographer's purpose to direct the visitor to different realms of specialist practice.

The signs you see attached to the hospital walls and hanging from the ceilings denote, on the one hand, technical expertise and the mastery of arcane skills. On the other, they are suggestive of depersonalisation, linked to the function, management and treatment of the body-as-machine, broken into constituent, interoperating parts. Just as the hospital itself is a jigsaw puzzle of fragments, so too is the approach of those who work there to the people requiring their services. In a respiratory ward, the focus is on the lungs above all else; the ear, nose and throat team are unlikely to be concerned with your broken ankle; you would not want a gynaecologist operating on your brain.

The experience at a small-town health centre is markedly different, even if the front-of-house bureaucracy remains the same. While there is still much for the senses to assimilate and absorb, one notable difference is the humanisation of the experience. Many of the signs that are visible offer the names of real people. These are the general practitioners (GPs) who are concerned with the whole human body rather than one minute part of it. The emphasis on medicine and treatment of the whole contrasts with the notions of localised surgical intervention and radiology that patients associate with the hospital.

Nevertheless, the domains of the health centre and the hospital are intimately connected. The journey of the cancer patient is most likely to start in conversation with the neighbourhood GP:

a discussion of recent anomalies and ailments, prompting short-term prescription and referral for tests. A gradual escalation process follows. The GP is not in possession of the deep knowledge required. They start from a position of not knowing, but they leverage both networked information and relationships, directing their patient into a system that will lead them to a specialist, expert in the narrow field relating to their particular category of cancer. A form of treatment is devised and acted upon. Rehabilitation will require the participation of other healthcare professionals, as well as the referring GP.

The patient's journey here illustrates the need for both generalists and specialists. It is never a question of either/or but both/and. Diagnosis, treatment and recovery require the input of generalist and specialist practitioners, spanning medical and surgical disciplines. It involves fluctuating moves from a big-picture, macro perspective to a narrow, micro one. Attention is paid to the whole person at a generalist, medical level. The specialist depersonalises, honing in on the malfunctioning organ, in order to let the care of the whole be resumed. The baton is handed off and passed back again. In healthcare there is clear delineation between general practitioner and specialist, covering the respective domains of medicine and surgery. Nurses and other medical professionals bridge between the two. Cooperation between all is essential to patient welfare in the case of serious illness and debilitating conditions. The edges are often blurred, however, in other arenas. The personnel frequently demonstrate both generalist and specialist tendencies. Labels become more problematic.

The institutionalisation of the label, and the constraints it demarcates, both physical and psychological, is an unfortunate legacy of the Industrial Revolution and its effects on society. The scientific management practices popularised at the turn of the twentieth century retain an insidious hold on how people think and organise themselves for manufacturing and knowledge work, even extending into healthcare and education. It is a dehumanised and mechanical approach that views individuals not as people with unique characteristics, knowledge and experience, but as replaceable parts. Their very humanity is occluded by the labels they are forced to bear. We remove this welder and replace them with that welder. When this accountant leaves, we will hire another accountant. Our project managers, nurses, teachers, bus drivers, are considered entirely interchangeable.

In the meantime, however, we have set up a conveyor belt of humanity that is geared towards squeezing people into the correctly shaped holes, ensuring that the label fits. Hyperspecialism is the end goal. The journey starts at school. We are sucked into a funnel at an early age. Educational choices made during our impressionable teen years can have a lasting effect. To select is also to exclude. Opting for certain academic disciplines during high school limits what can be pursued at university or as a trade. For those who aspire to it, a higher-education specialism then narrows workplace possibilities. Qualifications lead to employment, which in turn leads to the constraints of a role and job description; the path towards increasing functional expertise. Measurement and performance assessment impel us to sharpen our skill set within this restricted field. The myopia of the expert sets in. The boundaries within which the specialist operates get narrower still.

This funnelling has an inevitable consequence: it fosters silo-based practices and behaviours. Corporations, government departments, intelligence agencies and a host of other types of organisation bemoan the disjointedness of their departments, the lack of interoperability between IT systems, the hoarding and protection of knowledge. Yet this is the end result of a system that encourages hyperspecialism and narrow, deep expertise. Territories are demarcated and patrolled, as elsewhere in the animal kingdom, because personal or group survival may depend on it. This shortsighted and blinkered approach has a massive inhibiting effect when we shift our attention to the big issues that confront our society in the near, middle and distant future: population growth, increasing longevity of human life, healthcare, migration, climate change, conservation, natural disasters, food production, sources of energy, terrorism, military conflicts, the atomisation of work, different forms of economy and life beyond Earth, to name but a few.

Of course, nobody denies the necessity of specialism in the right context. Most people would prefer to have Jiro Ono preparing their sushi rather than a generalist short-order cook from the local diner. But the system is flawed. It has been skewed, with the result that the cult of the hyperspecialist has become the norm. One of our interviewees, Lucian Tarnowski neatly captures this discrepancy. He observes how it is socially acceptable to describe yourself as a specialist, in possession of deep skills and experience relating to a single discipline. Conversely, however, it is frowned upon to self-identify as a polymath, to promote and acknowledge your own serial mastery. It is a point echoed by Ella Saltmarshe who claims that she has often felt compelled to hide the diversity of her skills or risk being thought of either as a dilettante or as immature, suffering from Peter Pan syndrome. Polymathy is only spoken of in terms of aspiration rather than achievement; it is rarely acknowledged as a current state. Conceptually, it is perceived as challenging to the contemporary specialist mindset, as a threat rather than an opportunity. It belongs in the past, with the Renaissance.

What our research demonstrates, in fact, is that we all have the potential to both specialise and generalise, and that this potential is applicable across many aspects of life not just in the workplace. Take the example of rugby union, for example. The label *rugby player* is suggestive of a broad range of competencies and skills. Such an individual would be expected to be proficient in reading the game, attacking, defending, passing, tackling, catching and running. The label is generic and broadly inclusive. Other labels might distinguish between *forwards* and *backs*. Body shapes are somewhat different here, so too the likely speeds of players, their sleight of hand, their ability to kick the ball, their effectiveness in scrums, line-outs, rucks and mauls. The labels remain generic but less inclusive, with a stronger hint of specialism.

It is when the different positions in a team are explored that the concept of specialism, of expertise, fully emerges. The expectations and skills attached to the role of *flanker*, for example, are hugely different from those associated with that of *fly-half.* Richie McCaw and Dan Carter were both world-class players who experienced unprecedented success with the New Zealand All Blacks before retiring from the international game at the end of the 2015 Rugby World Cup. They were considered masters of the respective positions they played throughout their careers. But to have asked either one to take over the role of the other would have transformed them into a shadow of the player they were. While they would have retained the generalist capabilities of a *rugby player*, of a leader too, they would have been denied their specialist know-how and expertise as *flanker* and *fly-half* respectively.

In this sense, when McCaw took to the field wearing the number 7 jersey he did so simultaneously as both generalist and specialist – as a world-class rugby player and inspirational captain, and as a highly specialised open-side flanker whose effectiveness continued to mystify opponents and commentators alike throughout his fourteen years in the international game. To replace McCaw in the All Blacks team is not to lessen the team but to make it different, which is further suggestive of a particular expertise that defies anything as simplistic as a positional label.

In such a sport, generalism at a positional level, while useful to the team, is likely to confine the individual to walk-on parts from the substitutes' bench. The generalist rugby player who can demonstrate serial mastery in several positions is someone teams often turn to as the game enters its final stages. They cover numerous colleagues, replacing those who are injured, who underperform on the day or who demonstrate early signs of fatigue. Or they are introduced to effect a change in tactics. Their generalism, in such situations, is their strength, put wholly in service of the team.

Cycling is another sport in which individuals are required to both generalise and specialise. Road racing is a team sport in which only one person can emerge victorious. Context, including terrain, climactic conditions, team objectives and the specialism of each of the riders on a team, determines who will be supported by their teammates on any given day of racing. Cyclists, therefore, move fluidly through different roles, switching from their specialism to generalist duties as required. Many demonstrate mastery in more than one discipline. The contenders for overall victory in the Tour de France, for example, are expected to be among the best climbers in the race. Usually, high proficiency in time trialling is required too. A sprinter, on the other hand, can anticipate only a few days of potential glory and many days of suffering in such a three-week event.

Some cyclists are truly multidisciplinary. Nicole Cooke, for example, excelled as a junior cyclist on the road, in time trials, in cyclocross, in mountain biking and on the boards of the velodrome. However, Cooke realised that she was spreading herself too thin. To achieve her dream of becoming a professional road cyclist in the senior ranks, she accepted that she would have to become more specialised. Despite winning the national championship in cyclocross and being in contention to represent Great Britain at the World Track Championships, she opted to drop those forms of cycling from her schedule in 2001. Paradoxically, it was her generalist breadth that gave her the foundation to apply herself to specialist practice. The dividend was immediate for Cooke. In the same year, she earned a unique treble as the World Junior Champion in mountain biking, time trialling and road racing.

Further specialisation as a professional road racer culminated in 2008 with her dual victories at the Beijing Olympics and World Road Race Championships. Cooke took her generalist tendencies, her love of the bike and competition, and sharpened them into specialist expertise within a constrained field of endeavour. It is a story we see echoed in other walks of life: in business, in politics, in education, in the arts, in science.

As a young man, Paul Smith also aspired to a professional career in cycling, but he had to find new dreams and aspirations when injuries closed off that particular avenue. Discovery of art, graphic design and architecture, combined with experience in retail, led him to a life in fashion design and, latterly, photography. His entire career has been one informed by ongoing curiosity, creative inquiry, and magpie-like habits as a collector. As he suggests in the title of one of his books, *You Can Find Inspiration in Everything (And If You Can't, Look Again)*. Smith subscribes to the notion of lateral thinking. In the 1960s, when he developed an interest in Edward de Bono's ideas, Smith found himself part of a vibrant Notting Hill community in London that was beginning to make an impact on music, literature, art and fashion. A shift towards dandyism prompted his creative use of alternative fabrics, even as the traditional tailoring techniques of Savile Row were still being deployed. It is an important point. Ideas and inspiration were sought from all quarters, but traditional skills were still required to realise the new ideas. Creativity and innovation happened at the edge of what was already known.

Like Cooke in cycling and Smith in fashion, Saul Bass and David Byrne are examples of individuals who have elected to operate within a loosely defined domain – design and performance, respectively – but nevertheless have demonstrated polymathic tendencies across it. Bass was a graphic designer and accomplished visual storyteller. His career was one of constant border-crossings, finding expression in advertising, corporate logo design, children's literature, film posters and title credit sequences. He was adept at packaging an entire story into a static image, such as his poster for the 1958 psychological thriller *Vertigo*. The film sequences he made to open movies by Otto Preminger, Alfred Hitchcock and Martin Scorsese were masterclasses in how to complement and supplement the work of collaborators, anticipating narrative content and thematic motifs contained within their work. What was learned in the corporate world benefited what he created in the arts and vice versa. He could inject a diversity of skills and experience into whichever field he found himself in.

Byrne has wandered even more widely, drawing on his artistic and musical interests. Perhaps best known as the frontman of the band Talking Heads, Byrne has in fact worked across a breadth of musical genres, which he explores in his book-length exposition, *How Music Works*. He is also the author of *Bicycle Diaries*, a study of city life from the perspective of two-wheeled transportation. Byrne has enjoyed success as performer, composer, producer, author, curator, artist, photographer and filmmaker, winning multiple awards and collaborating with a host of luminaries in the fields of music, dance, opera and cinema. His range of experience and practice within the creative arts has been supplemented too by his business acumen. He is the founder of the Luaka Bop record label, for example, as well as an internet radio station. Byrne's curtailed art-school background and early experiences as a performer laid a firm foundation from which he could experiment and explore. His next move is always difficult to predict, arrhythmic like his stylised dancing, as he dodges the more obvious labels.

It is impossible to be a generalist all the time. Rather there are periods, time-bound and contextualised, during which people specialise, going deep, adding to their portfolio of skills and experience, before following their curiosity in another direction. Every polymathic generalist is, in fact, a serial specialist. Even as they become known for one thing, they are quick to demonstrate that they should be recognised for another too. Marie Curie, for example, was one of the pre-eminent scientists at the turn of the twentieth century. She enjoyed a multidisciplinary, border-crossing career that embraced both chemistry and physics, winning Nobel Prizes in each field. As well as developing a theory of radioactivity, she was responsible for the discovery of two new elements, polonium and radium. Her ongoing research contributed to medical practice too, including the development of X-ray equipment during World War I and a sterilising technique based on the use of radon.

There are many who find themselves in two places at once, flourishing in both, enjoying the experiences of combinatory play. Mori Ōgai, for example, became in 1881 the youngest person to earn a medical licence in Japan, going on to enjoy a lengthy career in his national army's medical corps, rising to the rank of Surgeon General. In parallel with his military life, Mori Ōgai was also a distinguished man of letters: a novelist, poet, biographer, translator and literary critic. Winston Churchill was a career politician, a statesman celebrated in particular for his leadership during Word War II. But he too was a writer, historian and artist, earning a Nobel Prize for Literature in 1953. Hedy Lamarr was a star of both stage and screen in her native Austria and latterly in Hollywood. She was also an inventor and applied scientist whose ideas and collaboration with George Antheil led to the development of a frequency hopping technique. This subsequently became a building block for modern technologies like Bluetooth, GPS and Wi-Fi. Frequency hopping, the perfect metaphor for the neo-generalist; wandering, accumulating, sampling, mixing, putting into practice what they learn.

Such people are uniquely difficult to categorise, defying classification systems. The ease with which they blur boundaries and cross borders undermines the very notion of classification. Dependent on your perspective, they can be seen to either label-dodge or label-accumulate, their presence in multiple places on the Linnaean system highlighting its flaws. Rather than finding themselves pinned in open-winged glory in a glass display case or squeezed into a narrow pigeonhole, they are to be found in flight. Mori Ōgai's progress up the military ladder can be understood in terms of his surgical competence and leadership. But such a narrow interpretation of his life would disregard his achievements in the literary world. It would present only half the man. Marie Curie's contribution to healthcare has to be interpreted in relation to the discoveries and advances she made in the fields of both chemistry and physics. Hedy Lamarr and George Antheil's invention owed as much to their shared love of music as to their scientific competence.

Labels stick only if we let them. The Myers-Briggs Type Indicator (MBTI) is a classic example. How many people have you encountered who passionately identify themselves with their MBTI label, transforming it into a self-fulfilling prophecy? How many others have you met who reject the label, question the methodology and highlight that it never represents who they are however many times they subject themselves to the assessment process? For the specialist, in fact, such labels may be a comfort blanket; for the polymathic generalist, the serial specialist, more often than not they are a nuisance, a hindrance. At best, they signpost where they are right now rather than where they have been, where they are headed, where they might return, where they might explore. There is always the danger, therefore, that the label is used to clip the individual's wings, to inhibit and prevent them from further flight. The pigeon must stay in its nest hole, not exploring the rest of the dovecote, let alone the outside world.

It is unfortunate that we can draw parallels between the lepidoptery collections of our natural history museums and the open-plan work spaces of the contemporary office or the assembly lines of the modern factory. In such settings, people embody facets of a different classification system, neatly categorised in terms of organisational functions. Stripped of their humanity, their individuality, these are people who are defined instead in terms of job titles, job descriptions and the placement of their role on the corporate hierarchy. They are victims of our need to label and pigeonhole, of the conundrum of taxonomy. They have been pinned to the cork board by a word or phrase; a reflection of the impulse to fragment and simplify. The label can apply equally well to the flesh-and-blood person who fulfils a function, as to an algorithm, app or robot arm that may be substituted for them.

The organisations and institutions where such labelling applies tend to have too many elevator shafts that permit movement only up and down, too few Willy Wonka elevators that 'can go sideways and longways and slantways and any other way you can think of'. We lack the interdisciplinarity, the multidisciplinarity, that results from mixing generalism and specialism. This can occur in the shape of a single person, as we will discover with many of the individuals who feature in this book. But it can also apply to couples in professional relationships like Warren Buffet and Charlie Munger, or in personal-and-professional relationships like Charles and Elizabeth Handy. It can apply to the composition of a diverse team, as witness successful sporting outfits like the All Blacks or the Team Sky road-racing squad. It is relevant to social and artistic movements, from the Bohemians of eighteenth-century London to the Modernists of 1920s Paris. It can also inform the operation and success of corporate ventures from the elastic enterprise of Apple to the federation of the Mahindra Group.

Replacing like with like, grouping the similar, denies us the opportunity to build bridges between different specialisms. It prevents us from sampling and mixing ideas from different areas of expertise. It diminishes our ability to innovate. It also constrains our development of dragonfly vision. This is the effect of multiple eye lenses combining kaleidoscopically to create a single holistic image, which Philip Tetlock and Dan Gardner describe in *Superforecasting*. People are excited by culinary mavericks like Heston Blumenthal and René Redzepi precisely because they look beyond the bounds of a traditional discipline, demonstrating a willingness to hybridise and experiment. Their work blends cuisine with art, with science, with environmental activism and sustainability. Their kaleidoscopes frequently refocus to serve up new patterns.

The neo-generalist, then, is *both* a generalist *and* a specialist, switching between the two as required. They are able to corral their generalist tendencies in service of deep specialisms. They generalise in order to specialise. Neo-generalists bring unique perspectives, blended knowledge and experience from diverse disciplines, to the specialisms they perform. But as lifelong learners and inherently curious people, they also demonstrate a facility in switching specialisms. When the context shifts, so do they. They are fluid and flexible. Their generalist preferences, when combined with what they have experienced through specialist activities, contribute to the development of metaskills: boundary-crossing capabilities that are essential as we respond to big issues or take advantage of unforeseen opportunities. In network terms, where a specialist can be thought of as living in a node and the generalist as occupying a liminal space on the bridges between nodes, the neo-generalist is in flow, constantly moving between bridge and node. They are adaptive, responsive, catalytic. While the specialist aspires to membership of the guild, populated by experts in their field, and the generalist heads for the salon, which is polymathic in both membership and outlook, the neo-generalist is drawn to a café culture in the hope of combining the best of both worlds.

Albert Einstein, for example, incubated ideas he had about physics and relativity, learning and conversing for years with friends from the informal Olympia Academy about philosophy, science and the arts, while he exercised a form of specialism assessing patent applications at the Federal Office for Intellectual Property in Bern. 1905 was a landmark year for him, as he began to put his new ideas and thought experiments about physics into the public domain via a series of articles and a PhD thesis. His context shifted as a result of what he himself had catalysed. As a consequence, he was able to mine his scientific speciality ever deeper, but also to connect with others from many different walks of life in academia, politics, film, music and other scientific disciplines. These connections and exposure to other fields shaped his own thinking and non-scientific endeavours, as evidenced in later publications such as *Ideas and Opinions* and *The World As I See It.*

Pablo Picasso also embarked upon deliberate intellectual and stylistic wanderings, whether at soirées hosted by the Steins, travels in Spain, or impromptu gatherings at bars, cafés or his Parisian home. Exposure to new ideas in other disciplines, including mathematics and poetry, prompted stylistic shifts and new forms of painting. Friendships and more intimate personal relationships inspired new directions, leading to formal experimentation and, with Cubism, the blending of artistic technique and ideas about geometry, space and time. One shift followed another, as curiosity and an ever-expanding network of friends and interests opened up new directions, new possibilities for artistic expression, not only on the canvas but in photography and sculpture too.

Picasso is a good example of the trickster-like capabilities of the neo-generalist. He operated in a liminal space, at the threshold of different domains that he served both to join together and to disturb. He could paint in the classical style but he could also challenge and overturn classical perspective, presenting a new way of seeing. He exploited the boundaries between different worlds, highlighting their porousness, allowing – actively encouraging – ideas from one world to infect another. We see something similar happening with the figure of the stand-up comedian, especially those who apply their talents in multiple fields.

Contemporary performers such as Eddie Izzard, Tim Minchin, Andi Osho, Ellen DeGeneres and Stephen Fry are our modern-day counterparts to the flâneurs of nineteenth-century Paris, observing and, peacock-like, being observed. They live in many worlds, either literally or figuratively, embodying questions of identity that relate to ethnicity, immigration, gender, sexual orientation, mental health and polymathy. They are stars not only of comedy clubs but of the stage, the screen, the radio and the bookstore.

These comedians draw on their own multiple perspectives of a subject to distort reality in a way that makes us laugh because of its simultaneous familiarity and absurdity. They too challenge us to see differently, shifting our mindsets and our view of what is around us. They educate even as they entertain. In an Ed Byrne show like *Outside, Looking In*, for example, despite its postmodern self-referentiality and ironic reworking of old jokes about bodily organs and functions, the audience members are forced to re-evaluate their middle-class lifestyles, their views about parenthood and gender equality. In Izzard's *Force Majeure Reloaded*, on the other hand, for all the surreal imagery, song-and-dance routines and multilingual play, the audience receives an historical overview of human thought and action that spans the period from the Ancient Greeks to the current period of unrest in the Middle East. Constantly, religious dogma, ideological zealotry and the effects of monarchical rule are exposed to ridicule, culminating in a call for modern-day wisdom of both leaders and followers.

The comic performers, through their border-crossing capabilities, are all translators, cage rattlers, influencers. The different media they make use of, from written text to camera to proscenium arch, serve as vehicles for their challenging ideas. Some are constantly pushing at the boundaries, mixing and sampling, experimenting. Minchin, for example, translates literary favourites into award-winning musical shows, bringing his own brand of rock comedy to children's fiction. Izzard has mastered the art of polyglot performance, delivering stand-up routines in multiple languages, drawing on his own hybridised cultural heritage. Many, like Stephen Fry and Sandi Toksvig, have found the panel quiz show a useful platform for combining their comic inclinations with the role of teacher. Dara Ó Briain is an intriguing case in point, not only partnering with other comics like Byrne to dissect current affairs on *Mock the Week*, but also drawing on his own academic background in mathematics and theoretical physics. To this end he has worked with Marcus du Sautoy, hosting *School of Hard Sums*, and with Brian Cox on *Stargazing Live*, an exploration of space, astronomy and physics. Here his comic persona is used as a means to make the difficult accessible, helping others to learn.

Lewis Hyde's *Trickster Makes This World* offers a useful key for unlocking some of the mysteries of the neo-generalist. His exploration of the trickster figure in the shape of Hermes and other mythological characters highlights a number of characteristics that are consistent with our ideas about neo-generalism. These include a comfort with ambiguity and the ability to move between different worlds, 'sitting in the middle of domains' as Jon Foster-Pedley, Dean at the Henley Business School South Africa, phrases it. The trickster serves as messenger, guide, translator, knowledge broker. They move back and forth from the edge to the centre, whether that involves descending from the gods to walk among the humans, or guiding others through the underworld. But they are also facilitators and teachers, even if in certain contexts they are known for their playfulness. This is certainly an analogy that applies to comic-educators like Izzard, Fry, Toksvig and Ó Briain.

It is also a trait that we have detected in some of the people interviewed for this book. Eddie Harran of the Deloitte Center for the Edge Australia is an intriguing example. He has developed an alter ego, Dr Time, which he uses to explore, share and work out loud as he examines and learns about humanity's approach to temporal concepts. During our research, we invited Eddie and many others to identify a metaphor that captured for them the concept of generalism. Several pointed to images that reflected ideas about bridging or connection or living in networks, from architectural structures to the paintings of Jackson Pollock. Nada Taha Borisly suggested an interesting variant: the Joker that since the 1860s has been found in a deck of playing cards. It is the wild card. An intriguing fusion of trickster and comic performer. Both the trickster and the neo-generalist traverse the spaces between polarities. They reconcile opposites. They demonstrate ambidexterity. It is a form of spectrum living.

The writer and illustrator Austin Kleon has published books titled *Steal Like an Artist* and *Show Your Work!* Together they demonstrate how people acquire knowledge and ideas from others, internalise and personalise them, then share their learning. The trickster both takes and gives. They go where the action is, then they inspire others to take action for themselves. The neo-generalist, like the trickster, mobilises their networked connections to access knowledge, to add to it, to keep it in motion, sharing with others. They practise the art of personal knowledge mastery, both teaching and learning. It is in the neo-generalist that multidisciplinarity and knowledge diversity coalesce. They collect, sometimes steal, knowledge from different domains, mixing and sampling in order to present new perspectives to these different fields. They move ideas from one discipline to another and thereby transform them. They too move others to action.

An interviewee for this book like Prasad Kaipa, therefore, takes his knowledge of physics, of energy and matter, and applies it to human relationships in his consultancy work. Susy Paisley-Day combines her expertise in conservation biology and her skill as an artist and textile designer to raise awareness of endangered species and to support charitable ecological initiatives in Latin America. Maggie MacDonald moves fluidly from performance art and writing to leadership education or environmental campaigning; from punk music to theatre to political negotiation. Henry Doss is able to combine musical composition and performance with an interest in history and archaeology and a role as venture capitalist and consultant. Bill Liao, another investor in start-up enterprises, serves as the co-founder of an organisation that helps children learn how to code, as well as a reforestation initiative that aims to reduce global warming by generating more cloud cover. Erika Ilves looks beyond the Earth's own atmosphere, exploring how resources can be mined, crops sustained, and life supported on other bodies in our own solar system and beyond. Closer to home, Carl Gombrich, Grace Clapham and Solonia Teodros put their own peculiar spin on the education system.

We will be meeting many other people in the second part of the book who typify the behaviours and characteristics that we associate with neo-generalism. These are creators, explorers, navigators, educators, meaning-makers. They demonstrate a form of serial mastery that, in *The Shift*, Lynda Gratton argues is essential for managing complexity and facing up to emerging problems and opportunities. But they undermine her notion that generalism is dead. As we will explore in more depth in the next chapter, both generalism and specialism, their fusion and hybridisation, are core to our notion of neo-generalism.

People like Prasad, Susy and Maggie demonstrate a facility in switching in and out of specialism and generalism as context dictates. Their personal preferences and inclinations are subsumed as they adapt to the environments in which they find themselves. Alone, deep specialists cannot resolve the world's big issues. In concert with neo-generalists, however, they give us all a better chance. We need those hyperspecialists to work alongside people who not only serve as connectors, bridging between disciplines, but who see the big picture and bring into play the metaskills that can help shape tomorrow's world.

2.
THE INFINITE LOOP

*The magic point where every idea
and its opposite are equally true.*

Donna Tartt, *The Goldfinch*

We tend to learn from nature because we are of it. In particular, we are drawn to the realms of animals, birds, fish and insects, studying their behaviours and actions, borrowing from them in our folk tales, mythologies, poetry, fiction, even our business literature. In a recent book, *The Meaning of Human Existence*, E. O. Wilson points to humanity's anthropocentricity, our fascination with both ourselves and others like us. We project our humanity on to other things, other creatures, in order to sense-make and explain. This is common knowledge for students of myth and human storytelling through the ages. It informs our understanding of narratives about Little Red Riding Hood's lupine encounters, Gregor Samsa's metamorphosis, Aslan's wanderings through Narnia and the adventures of Rat, Mole, Badger and Toad.

The attraction of metaphors drawn from the natural world applies as much to those who perceive humankind to be at the centre of the universe as it does to advocates of Gaia theory, who recognise the Earth as a self-regulating system and maintain that humanity has no more value or meaning than any other life form. The metaphors expose the porousness of boundaries, serving as bridges between apparently contrarian views. They are open to interpretation from a variety of perspectives, bringing personal context and subjectivity into play. Many are drawn to animal pairings, continuing a tradition that can be traced back to Aesop's tortoise and hare, via the satirist Jonathan Swift's bee and spider. Ori Brafman and Rod Beckstrom, for example, examine the organisational implications of the starfish and the spider, while Charles Handy highlights the differences between the elephant and the flea. From such studies we learn about human characteristics, decision-making capabilities, leadership style and communal preferences.

It is, however, through Charles's exploration of emergent change in business, highlighting the co-dependency of large organisations and multiple independents, that he casts a spotlight on another anthropocentric pairing. Charles underwent years of conditioning in the British education system before then being exposed to a complacent and traditional business world. Reflecting back on his experiences during the post-war decades, Charles observes in *The Elephant and the Flea*, 'I discovered later in life that I had been trained as a hedgehog when I was really a fox.' It is a recurrent theme in his writing. One that underpins his arguments about education and the portfolio life. Charles, the one-time classicist, is understandably drawn to a fragment of poetry from Archilochus. It has found its way into modern thought by way of the Renaissance scholar Erasmus's *Adages*. Isaiah Berlin subsequently adopted the ideas it contained to unlock his understanding of the work of Leo Tolstoy, helping popularise it further. *Multa novit vulpes, verum echinus unum magnum* (The fox knows many things, but the hedgehog one big thing).

Berlin's *The Hedgehog and the Fox* gave us the building blocks for exploring the differences and potential synergies between specialists and generalists. They have been co-opted and adapted by scholars and practitioners in a number of fields even if they have not always been informed by the pluralism that shaped Berlin's personal philosophy. Philip Tetlock, for example, in *Expert Political Judgment*, describes a twenty-year study exploring how successful people were at making predictions, and highlighting the distinctions between different character types on a hedgehog–fox continuum, including hedgefox and foxhog hybrids. Tetlock recognises that it is not simply a case of polarities with nothing in between. Instead, here and in *Superforecasting*, he observes that there is a whole spectrum, with subtle variations, between the two extremes. An individual might have natural inclinations in either direction, but context and the role they are required to fulfil can influence where they are positioned on the continuum at a given point in time.

*[**Figure 2.1.** The hedgehog and the fox]*

Tetlock's research has had a broad influence. This is evident, for example, in the work conducted by Peter Gomez and Timo Meynhardt at the University of St Gallen in Switzerland. They make a case for the complementarity of the respective strengths of the hedgehog and the fox, whether they are combined at an individual or a collective level. Their focus is on the environment of the boardroom, but their findings extrapolate to other fields too. Gomez and Meyhnardt also highlight other spectra that are collapsed into the different forms of thinking adopted by those with hedgehog and fox-like tendencies relating, for example, to differences between tradition and innovation, local and global, bureaucracy and autonomy, service and profit.

The hedgehog's steady, direct, single-minded pursuit of one right answer is contrasted with the speed, obliquity and curiosity of the fox. The hedgehogs depend on what is known, and have a conviction about the correctness of their own knowledge. They mine single subjects deeply. The foxes accept the boundaries of their knowledge, even as they seek to expand them, developing breadth of interest as well as depth. They are comfortable with ambiguity, believing that there is no single right answer. They embrace diversity of perspective. Foxes demonstrate the plasticity of an opposable mind, accommodating a form of trinitarian thinking. They are able to constructively assess and blend conflicting ideas

ts, overcoming the limitations of an either/or dialec-
at an array of alternative, enhanced options. As Prasad
rves, the differences between the hedgehog and the
te too the opposition of instinct and intuition. Instinct
belongs to the past and hedgehog-like tendencies. Intuition is more
future-oriented, reflective of fox-like behaviour and generalism.
Without intuition, Prasad argues, it is impossible to be a generalist.

In many respects, the notion of the hedgehog–fox or specialist–
generalist continuum is likewise a manifestation of this inclusive,
pluralistic approach. Either/or is replaced by both/and, embracing
the whole sweep of alternatives their hybridisation may offer. It is
an idea captured by Robert Pirsig in his *Zen and the Art of Motorcycle Maintenance*. Pirsig writes of a metaphoric knife, of analytical thinking, used to divide a handful of sand into parts. It is the
beginning of labelling, taxonomy and classification. He recognises,
however, that if the sand is observed closely enough, the rich variety presented by the different grains becomes visible. The viewer
makes out similarities and differences, and a continuum emerges
between what at first seemed two black-and-white polarities. For
Pirsig, the mindsets of those who are concerned with classified
and segregated heaps of sand and those who take a more holistic
approach are irreconcilable. Neo-generalism suggests otherwise.

The binary opposition of generalism and specialism is too simplistic. Evidence of difference is subtler, more complex. This applies
not only at an individual level but at a collective one too. It points,
for example, to the need for diversity in the composition of any
team or organisational structure. In *The Hedgehog, the Fox, and
the Magister's Pox*, Stephen Jay Gould expounds a brilliant thesis on why we need to bridge the gap between the sciences and
the humanities and do away with age-old misconceptions. He is
another to build a case for the hybridisation of the hedgehog and
the fox. Gould's book also highlights the taxonomical breadth of
the specialist–generalist continuum, the array of terms we have

dreamt up to categorise and label people, and the misunderstandings that have then evolved in relation to this terminology. What is particularly evident is the number of terms that have been developed to describe generalist inclinations and activities. This is suggestive of the difficulties generalists have had with making themselves understood in a world dominated by specialism.

Although it is itself a label, we view *neo-generalist* as an inclusive one that encompasses all those other terms that sit on the continuum. The neo-generalist is both specialist and generalist. Someone who moves along the continuum, adapting to context, even when personal preferences lean towards the extremes of fox-like behaviour. It is a point forcefully made by Bill Liao, Prasad Kaipa and John Michel in interviews for this book: context always outweighs personal preference. The generalist aspirant often has to operate as a specialist. Nevertheless, it is worth considering what some of these other hybridised terms are and what they mean. These are the different ports of call on the continuum. We need to develop a fuller understanding of each in order to arrive at a more rounded concept of the neo-generalist. In doing so, we can then largely dispense with these multiple variations and overlaps, relying instead on a single term. The starting point, however, is to double the length of the continuum. For the *hedgehog* and *fox* are but subsidiary terms in their respective specialist and generalist domains. At either extreme of the continuum stand the *hyperspecialist* and the *polymath*.

Key: **A** – Hyperspecialist **I** – Hedgehog **R** – Fox **Z** – Polymath

[*Figure 2.2. The continuum as line]*

Spacetime curves. Follow any line around the surface of the Earth and you will end up back where you started. With that in mind, we are intrigued by David Didau's challenge to bend dichotomies back on themselves. A fascinating thing happens when you transform the continuum into a circle. The hyperspecialist (A) and the polymath (Z) suddenly find themselves adjacent to one another. There is, on reflection, something reassuring about this. The hyperspecialist is a deep expert in a particular subject, often combining a wealth of theoretical and practical experience. The polymath is also a deep expert, only in numerous subjects. Their serial mastery manifests itself as hyperspecialism multiplied. Their adjacency, then, makes complete sense in terms of a cyclical continuum. So too the apparent opposition of the hedgehog (I) and the fox (R).

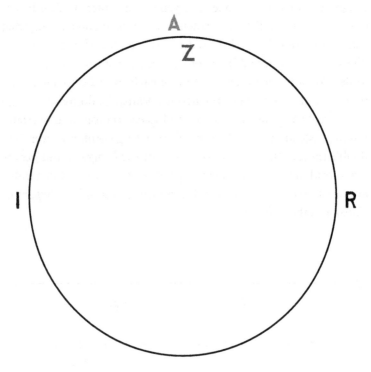

*[**Figure 2.3.** The continuum as circle]*

There is, however, a problem in both the linear and cyclical models in that they inadvertently suggest some form of step-by-step progression. This could not be further from the lived experience of either ourselves or the interviewees for this book. Travels along the continuum tend to be hyperlinked rather than progressive. A bit like jumping down a wormhole and reappearing elsewhere on the continuum as the context shifts. This is addressed by twisting the continuum, creating a Möbius strip or infinite loop. It is this that we have adopted as our visualisation of the neo-generalist. On the left lies the curve of specialism; on the right, that of generalism. At the centre the hyperspecialist and polymath nestle against one another, while the hedgehog and fox confront each other across the extremes of the continuum.

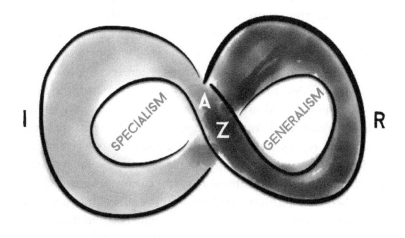

[Figure 2.4. The infinite loop]

What has become known as the *I-shaped* person or organisation is relatively easy to address. This is the hedgehog. An individual or collective who knows one big thing, developing expertise in that subject. As our alphabetical markings on the continuum suggest, moving back towards the letter A is suggestive of ever-deeper mining of this specialism. But each letter back towards A, each grain of sand, every floor on the elevator shaft, carries with it the dangers of silo-based thinking, of resistance to the influence of other fields and disciplines. This is not to suggest that this is always the incorrect approach, only to acknowledge its limitations.

The letter R we associate with the fox (or *renard* in French). The curve that runs from R to Z, however, also captures the notion of *Renaissance Man* or *Renaissance Woman*. This has become a loaded term and requires some unpacking. Gould, again, is incisive on this point. As he illustrates in *The Hedgehog, the Fox, and the Magister's Pox*, during the period we now know as the Renaissance there were a number of great philosophers and artists who looked back to and sought to revive the knowledge of the Ancients from Greece and Rome. They operated in the domain of the already known, but were not seeking to add to those knowledge banks. There was something hedgehog-like in their outlook and mindset. Conversely, in the realm of scientific endeavour, there were many figures who were challenging orthodoxy, religious faith, institutionalised power and our understanding not only of our own planet but the solar system of which it is part. They exhibited a fox-like curiosity, were modernist in their outlook, living with ambiguity and seeking to redraw the maps of what was known. What we have come to think of as a Renaissance person today, then, tends to embody a fusion of these two distinct groups, demonstrating a form of polymathic generalism that transcends the separation of the humanities from the sciences.

There are many other labels that have been applied to the figures that find themselves, however temporarily, situated on this R–Z curve. Chris Messina, for example, writes of the *full-stack employee*, although this is fairly narrowly presented from the perspective of the technology domain. Marci Alboher talks of the *slash career* through which an individual gives expression to multiple interests. One of our interviewees, Grace Clapham of the Change School, refers to herself as a *multi-hyphenate*, which is suggestive of the breadth and depth of her curiosity and expertise. In a variation on this, Emilie Wapnick of Puttylike describes the concept of *multipotentiality*. She uses her company as a platform for exploring and practising in a range of disciplines, embracing entrepreneurship, technology, digital nomadism, art and branding. Through her blogging and public speaking, she educates and guides others both on these subjects and on life as a multidisciplinarian, reflecting on both the positive and negative aspects of her personal experiences.

Another popular term for the notion of disciplinary breadth and depth is *comb-shaped*. Varying levels of competence, skill, knowledge and expertise across disciplines is captured by the modifier *broken*-comb-shaped. Following our alphabetical continuum, this type of individual or collective is captured by the letter W. Or, more suggestively, WWW, which reflects the idea not only of broad knowledge and expertise, as well as deep practical experience, but also the adeptness of the network navigator, finding their way in both the analogue and digital worlds. Through living in multiple worlds this type of polymathic generalist fulfils the trickster role, connecting, cross-pollinating, disrupting, guiding. They bring the concept of the *portfolio* person into the twenty-first century.

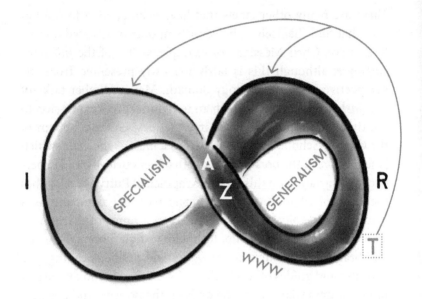

Key: **A** – Hyperspecialist **I** – Hedgehog **R** – Fox **T** – T-shaped person
WWW – Polymathic generalist **Z** – Polymath

*[**Figure 2.5.** Repositioning the T]*

The positioning of *T-shaped* people and organisations proves to be more problematic. Logic dictates – following the alphabet – that the T ought to be positioned somewhere between the R of the fox and the WWW of the comb-shaped. Certainly, that is how it has been advocated by the likes of Morten Hansen and Bolko von Oentiger in the pages of the *Harvard Business Review*, as well as by Tim Brown, the Chief Executive Officer of IDEO. But there is a problem in the very shape of the T: namely, the depth of the tail and the narrowness of the crossbar. Typically, a T-shaped person who follows a traditional career path tends to be one who develops and refines a deep specialism over time. Often this has a basis in their education, and is subsequently narrowed in focus as the subject is mined ever deeper. It is a practice that has become emblematic of the silos that many are keen to bemoan. The span of time and the deepening specialism ultimately results in promotion and the acquisition of managerial responsibilities. The I of the hedgehog is given a boss's hat.

It does not mean that the blinkers of specialism have been wholly removed. Responsibilities remain largely operational, drawing on the experience and deep knowledge of someone with subject expertise. Often it is the case that the broadening of a shallow skill set that is necessary for management is unsought and unappreciated, but that the constraints of career and promotion, the funnelling effect, render it the only way that high performers and subject experts can achieve appropriate remuneration. In times of difficulty, however, such as the financial crash of 2008, it is common for the T-shaped to withdraw to the tail, to the familiarity of their specialism and the myopia of their expertise. It is less common to find such people operating consistently at the top of the T, at the level of the crossbar, covering the breadth of managerial and leadership responsibility. When they do so, they are able to connect with peers in other disciplines in order to cooperate in finding solutions to big issues or scanning the horizon to take advantage of opportunities.

The T-shaped person, therefore, is invariably more specialist than generalist. They are more likely to be found operating at a level of deep specialism, only on occasion giving expression to a very shallow generalism. For this reason, it seems more appropriate to reposition the T elsewhere on the continuum, spanning both sides of the specialist–generalist curves. The T-shape is, in a sense, a continuum of its own that touches the top edges of both upper curves of the infinite loop: not quite at the level of hyperspecialist; only at the lower range of the generalist spectrum. There is a flickering as they switch back and forth between tail and crossbar.

Far easier to position is the *Pi-shaped*. This is an individual or collective with at least two deep areas of mastery, as well as a shallower range of generalist knowledge and experience that connects to other fields. The domain knowledge is broader with the Pi-shaped than with the T-shaped. They have not quite achieved the breadth of the fox nor do they have the polymathic generalism of WWW people. An O or P to the fox's R.

What this brief overview of the types demonstrates is that there is huge variety and interplay along the specialist–generalist continuum, encapsulating different facets of the neo-generalist. A quantum entanglement, of sorts. It would be misleading, therefore, to categorise any individual or organisation in terms of a single facet in perpetuity. In order to remain relevant, it is necessary to constantly adapt to context. The infinite loop is made up of fragmentary letters, countless grains of sand, a continuum of options. Only for time-bound periods do these collapse into a single selection. When the context shifts so does where we find ourselves on the loop. But so too how others perceive us. An individual can be a neo-generalist with many specialisms. Different observers will see only one of those specialisms and will label them accordingly. They impose their own classification system, wielding their analytic knives, using their filters to make sense of what they observe. This partially explains why someone can be understood to occupy many different places on the continuum.

It underscores one of the inherent difficulties for the neo-generalist. While an individual may feel they are giving expression to their generalism, others who have a different context, a different perspective, may see them as a specialist. Susy Paisley-Day, for example, can have clients who appreciate her art and craft, and understand her to be a new talent in the field of textile design. But that discounts her academic foundation and deep expertise in conservation biology, her experience in social enterprise or her passion for the people and ecology of Latin America.

Dependent on context, Tara Swart can be perceived as a leadership coach, an experienced medical practitioner or a neuroscientist. It is, however, when she combines the knowledge and experience from all these disciplines that she adds the greatest value to her clients.

Our term, the *neo-generalist*, then, acknowledges, encompasses and validates all these other terms. What we seek to challenge is the simplistic opposition of specialism with generalism. This is not about reductionism; it is about whole human beings. We also wish to reclaim other terminology from the clutches of negativity. Too often in this specialised world, words like *generalist, journeyman, curious, wonder* and *eclectic* are used in demeaning ways. People talk in derogatory terms of a *jack of all trades and master of none*, failing to understand that there is a progression, a continuous learning and practical cycle, that takes us from apprenticeship through journeyman status and on to mastery. As Ella Saltmarshe argues, they usually ignore the second couplet as well, undermining the positive connotations the term had in the Elizabethan era: *Jack of all trades / Master of none / Oft' times better / Than a master of one.*

The jack can often become master of many trades, skipping back and forth along the continuum, eclectic in their acquisition of knowledge and exposure to different experiences. The jack is a lifelong learner, a trickster who will acquire the skills to navigate through multiple domains. This is a badge of honour rather than a sign of inferiority. It is why this book is called *The Neo-Generalist* rather than *The Neo-Specialist*. It is about people who can specialise as the context requires it but whose personal preferences lie in the area of polymathic generalism, where they are able to exercise their curiosity and pursue diverse interests. They are a complement to those individuals who are specialists by choice, through the confluence of both preference and context.

What we learn from the continuum is that, as a rudimentary model, it has application well beyond our interest in the domains of specialism and generalism. Interviewed by the BBC in late 2015 about his role in *The Danish Girl*, actor Eddie Redmayne observed that the experience had taught him that there is a spectrum between notions of masculinity and femininity, and that not all people sit neatly at either end of that spectrum. The same applies in many other areas. We could design infinite loops, for example, that apply to introversion–extroversion, giving–taking, leading–following, fixed and growth mindsets, connectors, mavens and salespeople, and so on. Even the extremes of left- and right-wing political ideologies end up being remarkably similar to one another, manifesting as either fascist or communist dictatorships, cohabiting as the A and Z on yet another loop. Fundamentally, what these continuums teach us is that people rarely stand still. They move constantly and arrhythmically; they are adaptive and responsive. Trickster-like, they live in many worlds.

In the previous chapter, we suggested a network analogy: the specialist is found in nodes, the generalist on bridges between nodes, and the neo-generalist in constant flow, switching back and forth from bridge to node. The infinite loop visualises this sense of motion and restlessness. In the next chapter, we will use our own stories to illustrate these hyperlinked travels.

3.
A TALE
OF TWO
WANDERERS

Voracious in my appetite
For the uncertain and unknown

Charles Baudelaire, Congenial Horror

The maze and labyrinth are concepts, both spatial and meta-phoric, that were documented in Antiquity and popularised in the Middle Ages. They have retained their appeal, often used interchangeably, through the literature and art of modernism and postmodernism. The figure of Daedalus, for example, who designed the Cretan labyrinth that housed the Minotaur, resur-faces in James Joyce's 1922 novel *Ulysses*. Stephen walks the streets of Dublin, the city-as-labyrinth. In the same epochal year, T. S. Eliot revived the figure of Tiresias who sits at the centre of *The Waste Land*, his poem-as-labyrinth. In this figure, time, space and people converge: past and present, Ancient Greece and contemporary London, masculinity and femininity, vision and blindness. The labyrinthine tradition extends through the fiction of Borges, Calvino, García Márquez, Pynchon, Eco, Murakami and beyond.

The individual at labyrinth's centre is emblematic of personal journeys, personal narratives. Wherever I go, there I am. Where you go is who you are. It is always ourselves that we find in the middle of the maze. In his hero adventure, Joseph Campbell owes much to Carl Jung's ideas about individuation. He outlined a journey towards self-knowledge, an integration of the various aspects of an individual's personality as represented by differ-ent archetypal figures. A notion echoed in Abraham Maslow's progression to self-actualisation. Part of the journey requires that certain beasts – fears, misconceptions – are laid waste along the way. Crossing the threshold with Ariadne's spool in hand, requires movement into a liminal state. Old-world thinking has to be displaced.

It is impossible to remove ourselves from the sense-making pro-cess. Our modern labyrinths are the networks that we inhabit in both the physical and digital worlds. The nodes in the network become archetypal expressions of aspects of ourselves, our inter-ests, who and where we are. Because our vision is constrained by our own eyes and imaginations, we are always at the centre. We map our networks from ourselves. A friend mapping a similar network will find themselves at its centre too. Their map will differ from our own. It is impossible to escape entirely from our own perspective however much we may attempt to empathise with others, to reframe from where they are standing. Wherever we find ourselves, context and subjectivity both constrain and shape what we think and how we see.

RICHARD'S STORY

To be a randonneur, then, is to be a wanderer.
Someone on a journey, but in a somewhat random way.
The wanderer does not know his course, but discovers it.
The path discovers him, as much as he it.
Matt Seaton, *The Wanderer*

During my teen years, I used to bat away the inevitable question about what I wanted to be when I grew up with this stock response: 'An assassin. They are well paid, and they get to travel the world.' While such an answer was fuelled by the facetiousness of youth, it also betrayed my distrust of labels and neat pigeonholing. In my late forties, I still am discovering what I want to be, still learning who I am and where I belong beyond the safe haven of home and family. Belonging has as much to do with relationships, ideas and mindset as it does with notions of time and place.

Steve Jobs once observed, 'You can't connect the dots looking forward, you can only connect them looking backwards.' This is an observation that resonates with most people given to wandering, whether that is through the physical ambulations of the flâneur or the even less constrained roaming of the mind. What in the act of living can appear circuitous and fragmentary, in memory's reconstruction can be shaped into a coherent narrative. We humans are ever sense-makers, always storytellers. Our memories, as James Sallis phrases it, are more poets than reporters. Elliptical, metaphoric, abstract, symbolic. Their realities ones of contextual convenience rather than necessarily lived experience.

As I reconstruct them, then, my early years were somewhat itinerant, leaving me with a sense of rootlessness. By the time I was ten years of age, I had started life in rural Yorkshire, spent four years in south-eastern Spain both on the coast in Mojácar and in the city of Murcia, then moved to an Oxfordshire market town where my parents set up a business. My schooling experiences to that point were equally disjointed, some of my stays lasting little more than a week. Friendships were transient, all too quickly left behind. An experience exacerbated in my early teens when my closest friend lost his life in a tragic household accident. Little wonder, then, that from an early stage in life I cultivated the position of an outsider. I expected impermanence. Best to observe and learn before moving on again, even as I railed against the moves, the constant change, the potential loss of treasured possessions, valued relationships. Settling in to a second Oxfordshire home for the next decade of my life did little to alter this outsider's perspective. School and friends were elsewhere. The only tenuous connection I had to the local community was through the nearby rugby club.

It is the recollection of time spent in Mojácar that is idealised in my mind's eye. Memories of the sandy expanse of beach below where our family home was perched on the side of a hill; of fish landed and sold at the local harbour in Garrucha; of the prevalence of índalo iconography; of film-set playgrounds that

I subsequently learned were left over from the Sergio Leone spaghetti westerns I would grow to love later in life. But I also recall my first exposure to the institutions of formal education at this time. I was a non-Catholic Anglo attending a school run by strict nuns in Franco's authoritarian Spain. An outsider again. My reaction was visceral and it shaped my response to the classroom setting for the next fifteen years or so. In fact, it would not be until I returned to Spain for a year as an undergraduate at the University of Zaragoza that I fully began to appreciate my academic potential and the scaffolding that could be provided by established centres of learning.

In the intervening years, back in England, I encountered Catholic nuns again who instilled in me not their faith but a deep sense of guilt. Between the ages of ten and thirteen, my happiest educational experiences were at a local private school. The Elizabethan house where we studied and slept, the broad curriculum and, above all, the emphasis on sports and the great outdoors all contributed to my appreciation of those years. Grammar school and a very different approach to education followed. This was my first taste of life as a commuter, with a two-hour round trip by bus each day. Rugby again was the raft I clung to, as I otherwise was manoeuvred along the fast-moving educational torrent, shaped, conditioned and smoothed by the water's flow.

The objective was the accumulation of certificates. Examinations were taken early, qualifications secured, in order that yet more examinations could be squeezed in. The deep shafts of specialism were being assembled. Constraints were in place too, either through exclusion or selection. Given my childhood, it was understandable that Spanish was a favoured subject. Interestingly, however, I never had much aptitude for its study as a language, speaking and writing it, but was more interested in the cultural elements: food, history, literature and film. Latin would have offered a useful complement, but I was not permitted to study it as my mathematics were not strong enough. In its place, I was compelled to take biology, as well as having to choose between history and geography, when I would have liked to spend more time with both.

Today, I retain nothing of the experience of formal scientific study. Rather it was the deep exploration of literature and film history while at Zaragoza that opened my eyes to the potential of science. It was through the humanities that I gained understanding and appreciation, not through the seemingly endless hours in the science laboratories at grammar school. Modernism and its successors expanded what I knew and the places I looked for inspiration. That year in Zaragoza was seminal in my personal development. Until then, I had played the game, collected the certificates, experienced both success and failure. A difficult decision at eighteen had paved the way. A surprisingly mediocre result in one subject prompted me to spend an extra year as a schoolboy. During that period, I mixed part-time study with temporary employment, determining that rather than going on to study law as originally intended, I would continue with Spanish for a few more years. My first year at Newcastle University raised questions about the wisdom of that choice. School had spoon-fed. I now needed to work out for myself how to learn.

Experiments in my second year at Newcastle, exploring beyond the curriculum, helped lay foundations that the experience of studying in Spain then built upon. By the time of my return to Newcastle for the final year of my degree, I knew that I wanted to research film history at postgraduate level. Zaragoza had given me the confidence to go both deep and wide, to combine different disciplines, to follow my curiosity. I experienced the benefit of mentoring from young, enthusiastic academics, as well as a crash course in film history at the local filmoteca that I sometimes visited twice a night. Comparative literature made me appreciate familiar texts in a completely new way. Discussion of theory and philosophy made sense in ways they had not done previously. Learning in my twenties was suddenly fun and rewarding. Being in a certain place at a certain age had the happy effect of completely shifting my mindset, developing an appreciation for lifelong learning that has little to do with the institutional conveyor belt of our formative school years.

Largely, this was because I was now investing so much of myself in the act of learning. I was no longer being done unto, offering up my mind unquestioningly to others like a sausage casing waiting to be filled with meat. Instead, I was engaged and active in the process of learning. I was looking a few steps ahead now too, wondering whether academia was a place where I might belong. The possibility of researching deeply into a subject, of hyperspecialising, was appealing. Especially if that could lead to an academic career, further writing and research, and the opportunity to mentor and guide others in the way I had been in Zaragoza. By the time I returned to England, I had already determined a topic to research for a PhD thesis. I began to live in two academic worlds, completing my undergraduate course on Spanish and Latin American studies even as I started to research the history and evolution of American film noir in the context of industrial, socio-political and cultural change.

As it transpired, I spent the bulk of my postgraduate years away from Newcastle University, where I was affiliated to the Department of English Literature. As a film specialist, I needed to be closer to the British Film Institute's facilities in London. I quickly fell into the solitary life of the writer and researcher. An outsider, an exile, once more. When I did have opportunities to teach, I disliked the expectation that I was all-knowing, ready to impart knowledge and receive nothing in return. This was not the kind of mentoring, not the hoped for mutual development, that I had had in mind. Once I had graduated, I strayed from the academic path and found myself in the freelance publishing world mostly editing, sometimes writing, even fulfilling one of my childhood ambitions to see my own book in print.

The most interesting work at this time, though, tended to be the side projects rather than the paid assignments. Some of these involved self-education, picking up HTML and CSS skills, for example, or making initial forays into information architecture and user experience. Some involved the occasional writing experiment. On the back of my research into post-World War II US history and culture, I had developed a fascination with crime fiction, particularly with examples that challenged conventions and bridged the boundaries between genre fiction and literary modernism. The discovery of James Sallis's oeuvre was significant for me, appealing to the latent scholar as I produced an article on his Lew Griffin novels, as well as the apprentice coder as I dabbled with various iterations for a website to showcase the man and his work.

It was an important lesson too in how internet-based technologies could enable connection, helping establish a new friendship, making accessible and humanising the name that adorned the covers of the books I admired. While researching my book on film noir, I had enjoyed the occasional frisson of excitement as I exchanged letters and faxes with the great and good of the cinematic past. With Jim Sallis, I enjoyed the more regular interaction that email enabled. Social media subsequently served to amplify these effects, breaking down barriers, improving both accessibility and immediacy of interaction. Invariably, I find myself now reading a new book and simultaneously interacting with its author on Twitter, perhaps simply expressing thanks, occasionally pursuing a line of thought that their work has inspired.

As I diversified during these post-academic years, first as a freelancer, then through a series of roles with private, public and non-profit organisations, it was fascinating to discover how those postgraduate experiences stayed with me. They were both foundation and touchstone. Whatever your generalist inclinations, academic research is a form of hyperspecialism. The joke goes that PhD stands for 'piled high and deep', suggestive of the individual's mining of an ever-narrowing field. They learn more and more about less and less, blinkered about what they do not know, disconcertingly satisfied with what they do. The trick is to learn how to apply the knowledge gained in different contexts, occasionally opening the way to new insights and innovation.

Writing and research were obviously portable skills. But I also found that I retained an aptitude for learning, as well as for translating the new knowledge that I acquired into something that could be shared with others too. Study of a visual medium gave me an understanding of on-screen communication, which overlapped with ideas relating to user experience and design. Storytelling and an understanding of culture – embracing history, semiotics, anthropology and psychology – were all vital to the ways in which I made sense of the world around me. In a workplace context, where I might be surrounded by web developers, health professionals, scientists, regulators, civil servants, policymakers or engineers, it gave me a different perspective, a different lens. It helped me understand that the role of an outsider could be a position of strength, one that could benefit the organisations I worked for. It was the conduit to external ideas, transcending corporate, industrial and national boundaries, opening up the possibility of cross-pollination. It was a case of learning how to navigate different networks, mapping them in order that others could follow.

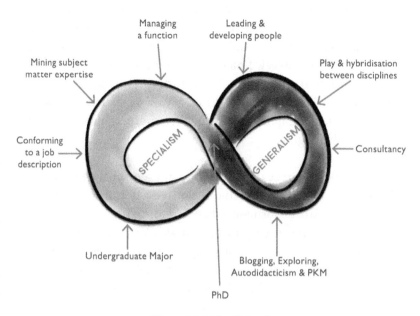

Managing a function

Leading & developing people

Mining subject matter expertise

Play & hybridisation between disciplines

Conforming to a job description

SPECIALISM

GENERALISM

Consultancy

Undergraduate Major

Blogging, Exploring, Autodidacticism & PKM

PhD

*[**Figure 3.1.** Richard's loop]*

In *Flawed but Willing*, coach and facilitator Khurshed Dehnugara differentiates between the teacher as expert, representative of the industrial age, and the community as expert, which is more characteristic of what he calls the age of connection. This resonates with my personal experience as an academic. In the 1990s, I developed deep expertise regarding film history and the noir genre in particular. I spent countless hours watching relevant films. I read about the topic, I wrote about it, I taught courses about it. By the end of the decade, however, I had left academia. Today, I still retain a keen interest in cinema and film history, still write about it on occasion, weaving references to it into my work on business, change, leadership and learning.

However, I am no longer what could be thought of as an expert in the field. Instead, I rely on networked connections, access to other people, their ideas and published work, to maintain some currency in the subject. I may not have the answers but I know who to turn to if I need them. The knowledge, the expertise, is in the network. It is always in motion. My own expertise, unused, has atrophied. Temporary residence transforms into a sense of no longer belonging.

This has been a recurrent theme in my personal experience. Knowledge withers if the vine is not tended and watered. My Spanish remained dormant when I returned to the UK as a child, but I found it easy to relearn as a teenager after a seven-year hiatus. But I have lapsed again since my undergraduate days, and would find it difficult now to hold my own in conversational Spanish without immersing myself in the culture for a period of time. Over thirty years since I last played, I would struggle to produce anything melodic on a guitar, while musical notation has lost all meaning for me, nothing more now than blobs on the page, birds on a telephone wire. New knowledge, though, can soon lead to expertise. Working in the health sector in adulthood, for example, it was necessary for me to rapidly gain breadth and depth in the theory and practice of information governance. This shaped my work, my behaviour and who I was required to be in the office for a number of years. I again became an expert in a narrow discipline, practising it, guiding colleagues on it, cooperating with other experts outside my own organisation.

An interesting experience during this time was when I opted to pursue a master's degree in information rights. I quickly dropped out, realising that I was gaining far more useful knowledge and experience through what I was doing in the workplace than in any of the interaction with the course leaders, who only knew the theory. Who needed another certificate to validate what they were doing on a daily basis? Nevertheless, this form of deep specialism was restrictive. It imposed a label on me, a workplace identity, that I struggled to escape. However much I might protest that in addition to *this*, I was also *this*, I had been categorised and pigeonholed by those who surrounded me. The option was either to move on, to change my specialism, or to buy into the masquerade. That would require continuing to perform, getting into character as the subject expert, checking most of my interests, much of my personality, at the door before entering the workplace each morning.

At one job, I used to have to commute by car every day along the concrete and asphalt arteries that connect Kent to London. I often found myself caught up in the experience of travelling at velocity but feeling like I was moving in slow motion. This is the effect of all the vehicles surrounding you moving at the same speed. As you become conscious of the phenomenon, your focus shifts and you become more attuned to those around you. It is not unlike one of those special effects seen so frequently in television advertising, where the protagonist occupies an oasis of calm while all around them is a blur of frenetic motion. It is an apt metaphor for the manner in which we can shift repeatedly from generalism to specialism, from self-contained silos to border-crossing wanderings. People occupying the narrow lanes of subject matter expertise race towards the acquisition of more experience and knowledge in their chosen field, only dimly aware of others outside their lane as streaky blurs in their peripheral vision. I longed to be the brave soul who opts to change lanes, to alter their pace, to explore elsewhere. To move from fast to slow.

My own wanderings have taken me from academia to publishing, from web consultancy to corporate governance, from rural furniture manufacture to the centre of the City, from health to transport, from a dot-com start-up to the public sector, from knowledge management to change leadership, from writing to mentoring. Context has determined to what extent I have been able to generalise or specialise. Web consultancy, for example, required a breadth of skills but little depth. Client liaison, information architecture, user experience, technical specifications, content management and some coding were all part of the mix. It was a facilitative role, a bridge between internal developers and external customers, understanding and translating the needs of each. The role of a trickster-like messenger. Information governance in the IVF sector, on the other hand, demanded deep specialism in a quasi-legal role. Context shifts triggered by job changes, redundancies, revised legislation, economic crashes, new governments, simple curiosity for alternative ideas, for new knowledge, demand parallel shifts on the specialist–generalist continuum. I have had to work as a hedgehog, as a T-shaped person, as a hyperspecialist, even as I have had to suppress an inclination towards, and preference for, the foxiness of the polymathic generalist.

Working as an independent is where I feel I have been able to give most expression to that polymathic tendency. My workplace is wherever I happen to be: my home, the saddle of my road bike, local cafés, the beachfront, art galleries. My clients are dispersed, living and working in other countries, other time zones. The assignments are varied. Conversely, however, it is in those roles *within* organisations, operating as an outsider on the inside, where I believe I have been of most effective service. For a brief period, I was a school governor, acting as a critical friend to the teaching staff and administrators. It is that ability to constructively challenge, to be in many worlds at once, introducing knowledge and ideas from elsewhere into a different context, where I feel my neo-generalism has been most beneficial to the individuals and the organisations I have worked with. On occasion, however, I have had to take a Trojan Horse approach, withholding my multidisciplinarity until others have grown comfortable with me in relation to a given specialism, only gradually revealing other capabilities and interests that can add value.

Tied in with this is a strong personal belief in the notion of transformational leadership, in preparing the ground for others, supporting them, transferring skills where relevant and, ultimately, making myself redundant. It is leadership as a form of service. A consigliere, rarely in the spotlight, often in the shadows whispering in a well-chosen ear. I also am a firm advocate of both individual and collective responsiveness, of adapting fluidly to the contexts in which we find ourselves. It is not in business literature or corporate training programmes that I have learned about these things. Instead, it has been through practice, experimentation, reading fiction and poetry, watching film and sport (especially rugby and professional cycling), enjoying the benefits of parenthood, and through interaction with friends and family.

I understand now that as a neo-generalist my role is to help others appreciate what they do and where they find themselves. This is the role of mentor and guide stripped of its scholastic trappings, informed by personal knowledge and experience. My personal story has threaded through it an academic theme because at heart I retain a desire to teach, to continue learning, to follow my curiosity and to maintain the sense of wonder I appreciate so much in my own children.

KENNETH'S STORY

I keep six honest serving-men
(They taught me all I knew);
Their names are What and Why and When
And How and Where and Who.
I send them over land and sea,
I send them east and west;
But after they have worked for me,
I give them all a rest.
Rudyard Kipling, The Elephant's Child

What do you do? Like many others, I find it hard to answer this question briefly. When asked, I usually tell people that I live in more than one world. Kipling's six honest servants are also my allies. These interrogative friends invite me into people's lives and help unearth their stories. As a thinker, writer, speaker, adviser and educator, I seek to address the most important questions in life. What drives you? Why do you care? When do you show up? How do you learn? Where are you heading? Who are you? By exploring these difficult questions with people, I learn about myself. By telling other people's stories, I tell my own.

Life has its ways of sneaking up on you. I am an existentialist who grew up with little practice in questioning the status quo. Raised in a harmonious atmosphere in small-town Denmark, there was no great urgency to play at the edges. My parents were ever-present for my sister and me, running their independent accountancy company. Frejlev, a satellite community near Aalborg, was the kind of place you could cycle through in two minutes. A tightly-knit system of suburban paths connected nearly 1,500 people, two small supermarkets and a local school. Our neighbourhood was comprised of young families, the source of numerous playmates. When someone died, got into trouble or excelled, everybody knew about it the next day. Few people wanted to stand out and be the news. It was not until later that I would abandon routines, wander and let go of the constraints.

My parents read me many stories, exposing me to the magical world of fiction. Stories by Hans Christian Andersen, Astrid Lindgren, A. A. Milne, Kenneth Grahame, Ib Spang Olsen and Tove Jansson were frequent bedtime companions. When I learned the alphabet I took matters into my own hands and befriended Asterix, Tintin, Lucky Luke and Spirou. Later, I included Sherlock Holmes, Robinson Crusoe, Robin Hood, The Three Musketeers, Long John Silver and Aragorn in the circle. My love of language unconsciously gravitated me towards a universe inhabited by outlaws, explorers, tricksters and detectives. The presence of imaginary friends who knew how to solve a puzzle, command a ship, throw a punch and challenge the status quo was a constant source of inspiration.

In the late seventies, television introduced me to the expeditions of Jacques Cousteau and Thor Heyerdahl. Both were men of wide-ranging interests that led them to push the boundaries of established science. These explorers opened up a new world to me. My grandfather, who had spent most of his working life as a chief engineer aboard freight ships, was my guide into this unfamiliar territory. In his presence, I would while away the time studying maps and listening to stories of exotic and far-away places. This further nurtured a desire in me to explore unbeaten paths.

At the age of thirteen, I got a job cleaning parking lots at a supermarket in a neighbouring town. This was the first of many jobs that I held as a teenager and it introduced me to the concept of leadership. Most of my jobs were of the blue-collar variety, involving an instructional and scaffolded approach to learning. Newcomers were expected to keep quiet, observe and emulate their colleagues. Questioning things and voicing ideas were not part of the routine. As a teenager, I worked at local factories, hotels and supermarkets, while also being exposed to the military through a work placement in school. I was a beginner many times over, mostly learning from things that I did not like. Observing managers with no passion for people taught me how behaviours take shape in organisations. I discovered that I had an unflinching sense of social justice as I often got into situations where I would defend and look out for the interests of others. *Treat people like you want to be treated* became my leadership mantra.

In my youth, I was never passionately committed to only one thing. I loved sports and actively engaged in tennis, swimming, skiing, badminton, judo, running and handball. But the constant source of camaraderie and play was football. I found that the position I was best suited to was that of goalkeeper. *Guardian, lighthouse, outsider.* Those are common labels attached to goalkeepers in football. A goalkeeper's place is in the middle of the woods, as Albert Camus described it. The space I defended, between the ages of five and eighteen, was eight feet high and eighteen yards wide. As goalkeeper, I was both a member of the team and somehow set apart, working in solitary as a specialist. I wore a different coloured jersey to my teammates, adhered to additional rules and had to operate in my own designated section of the field. For the most part, training was an isolated affair too. In his 1906 publication, *The Book of Football*, the Welsh international Leigh Richmond Roose observed that a successful goalkeeper, like the silkworm, must produce his materials from himself unless he wishes to be purely imitative.

Fast footwork and reaction speed are essential for a goalkeeper, but the hallmark of the best number ones is their ability to think ahead and imagine the future. I learned that from spending hundreds of hours poring over and replicating the actions of

Liverpool's Ray Clemence. He moved in response to the world. He was a skilled forecaster and assimilator of the game, which allowed him to leap into action at the right moment. You are on your own as a keeper, and the margin between victory and defeat is slim. A step to the side is all it takes to either mess things up or save the day. You constantly try to calculate angles and position yourself for the opponents' next move. In its essence, goalkeeping is the art of mastering juxtapositions. You are still most of the time, then you burst into action in order to manage crises. You are both observer and participant, responding to context, communicating your vision and needs with varying levels of urgency dependent on the threat posed by the opposition.

In *The Goalie's Anxiety at the Penalty Kick*, Peter Handke eloquently describes how nervous tension is a constant in a goalkeeper's life. Despite playing football to a high standard, I never had to endure the burden of being on live television, exposed to media attention or the expectations of a large crowd that are part of the baggage of a professional career. But I still experienced different forms of pressure brought on by competition, not only in matches with opposition teams, but internally within the squads I was part of. My fondest footballing memories are from my last year as a junior player when I switched from the local club to a larger one in the main regional city. There I faced the rivalry of two colleagues who were also chasing the club's No. 1 jersey and a place in the team's starting line-up. That year I discovered how far a clear focus and perseverance within a narrow field can take you in sports.

Exposure to formal education was equally enjoyable. My mind was receptive, especially when a subject interested me. But I was easily bored once I understood a topic. The tension that came from experiencing things with a fresh perspective was a driving force for me. Quite foolishly, I saw every maths test, essay or sports activity as an opportunity to express my competence.

It was never about winning but rather a matter of accomplishing a goal and having it validated by others. As I advanced into upper secondary education, I was not ready to specialise, opting for the generalised three-year academic programme offered by the Danish Gymnasium. There I found myself academically challenged in a broad range of subjects in the fields of the humanities, natural sciences and social sciences. I graduated with an advanced certificate in mathematics and natural sciences, but I had no idea yet what I wanted to do in life, choosing to supplement my studies with a one-year Higher Commercial Degree to get a taste for IT, law and accounting. That is how I met Thomas.

Thomas and I shared a deep desire to travel and explore. We committed to save up enough money to backpack our way around the world, which saw me working simultaneously at a kindergarten, petrol station and supermarket. Our first stop, in January 1994, was Los Angeles. As we celebrated our first night away from home, a strong sensation of freedom mixed with anxiety set in. It was a realisation of having placed ourselves in an unpredictable situation, an ambiguous space, where we had to make meaning every day, roll with the punches and learn to adapt.

Books and conversations were our primary tools for navigating unfamiliar roads while away. I learned that maps and guides are useful but never complete. Once your feet are on the ground things seldom work the way you imagined. Maps give us the illusion of control, a sense of direction. There is a difference between way-keeping and way-finding, as Lynn Darling writes in *Out of the Woods*. The first relies on sticking to a certain path and following well-marked landmarks, while the latter draws on following an inner compass, paying attention to the landscape and being willing to alter one's route. Backpacking was a way-finding process that reversed the learning principles I had been exposed to in educational institutions by emphasising experimentation before reflection and theory in that order of importance. I found that my accumulated knowledge was being tested in my actions during difficult situations. A passport full of stamps can be just as valuable as any certificate from an elite institution.

Rather than follow the academic path to become either a teacher or lawyer upon my return from the world trip, therefore, I was soon relocating to Spain with another friend, Nicolai, to acquire a new language. I learned Spanish in a playful way, co-creating with my teacher, building a curriculum around my passion for football. This was my sixth language, another key to unlock and appreciate cultural nuances. Linguistic knowledge undresses cultural codes, norms, behaviours and aspirations, exposing their anatomies. My international travels transformed me into a wandering spirit in search of identity. Like Ishmael in Herman Melville's *Moby-Dick*, I developed an itch for new lands, a desire to see with fresh eyes. For fifteen years, I measured my life in suitcases. Rootlessness was my only real permanence. I fought a mental battle between here and there. Yesterdays and tomorrows. Goodbyes and hellos. Wanderlust still burns in me but I have accepted that home is many places, not only geographically but also professionally and mentally.

I continued to dabble with formal education too. I explored drama, philosophy, literature, dance, psychology and outdoor sports at a folk high school targeted at adult learners. A short stint at Copenhagen Business School also offered me a chance to dive deeper into economics and languages. But it was not until I attended a preparatory course to become a journalist that I found my specialism. My dream was to become a foreign correspondent. This would allow me to combine my love of stories and exploration. It also spoke to an idealistic impulse to inform others while doing good in the world.

Wisdom begins in wonder, said Socrates. So did my first week at The Danish School of Journalism. Our teacher told us to walk the local streets with one sole purpose: be still and see. We were supposed to let our senses wander, detecting the odd and the intriguing. I was trained in what psychologist Howard Gardner refers to as searchlight intelligence. That is, the ability to discern connections across spheres, bringing people and ideas together, where others see no possible connection. I became fluent in seeking information, making sense of it and sharing it. Journalism is, at its best, a craft that draws on a student's curiosity and a teacher's wisdom: novelty and experience combined. My interest is sustained by the tension between these forces. What unites them for me is common sense and a healthy scepticism of all things constructed, spanning ideas, viewpoints, religions, organisations or politics.

I had mastered a craft, yet I found that it was not an occupation that appealed to me. A short foray into the world of public relations, however, prompted a rethink. The agency I worked for had strong political ties and excelled in shady deals and dodgy favours. The clients were mostly titans of the pharmaceutical industry who would go to great lengths to sell more drugs by influencing decision makers and GPs. I was faced with an ethical dilemma, electing to leave after only ten months. The experience prompted me to explore becoming a foreign correspondent in India, where I would stay in Mumbai with my friend Lars who was based there working on a World Bank project restoring the sewage system. This would be the beginning of an enduring love affair with India. Although an experienced traveller, initially I was overwhelmed by a genuine culture shock. It is impossible to be indifferent in India. A curious mind and attentive heart gorges on the multiple contrasts that the country serves up. India grew on me and I have returned to visit and learn from her many times since.

Selling stories as a freelancer from India was problematic. With the benefit of hindsight, there were two reasons for this.

First, I did not have deep and trusted relationships with editors in the media industry. Second, the timing was wrong as India would not strengthen its economic position on the world stage until a few years later. I see it as a recurring theme for neo-generalists. We live on the edge of the future and detect signals early on by accessing a wide variety of people, ideas and information. But to benefit from this sensitivity, you need the support of people who are ready to engage and the patience to act when the moment is right.

Back in Denmark, I was determined to draw on the combination of these travelling, educational and work experiences, designing my own work. Again, I was grateful for the support of friends. Anners directed me towards a company in the leadership industry that had been honoured as the best place to work in Denmark. To my surprise they barely had a public voice. After a month of research, I sent them an unsolicited report with observations and suggestions for how they could showcase their knowledge and usefulness through storytelling. This was a deliberate attempt to carve out a new role as a knowledge broker rather than a PR specialist. The company's senior managers had faith in me, offering an opportunity to experiment with this new approach.

The business grew as I specialised in leadership and management storytelling. Soon I also found myself working with international business schools as their knowledge broker in Scandinavia. For more than a decade, I attended a wide range of courses, seminars, conferences and MBA programmes related to leadership. Fortunately, I could choose any subject that I found interesting in domains like neuroscience, psychology, innovation and design thinking. Like art, knowledge brokering is not only a question of what you can see but also what you can help other people to see.

Knowledge brokers build bridges between people and ideas by being exposed to many different specialities. They challenge the restraints of specialists and enlarge their imagination by exposing them to alternative ways of knowing, doing and being. As an independent knowledge broker, I spent a lot of time asking questions and listening in the organisations I worked with. It was a process of gathering and conceptualising stories, connecting with people, scouting for useful knowledge that could showcase their expertise. I ended up writing and producing 300 stories on a yearly basis in media outlets worldwide. The majority of them addressed how emerging trends would influence individuals, organisations and society as a whole.

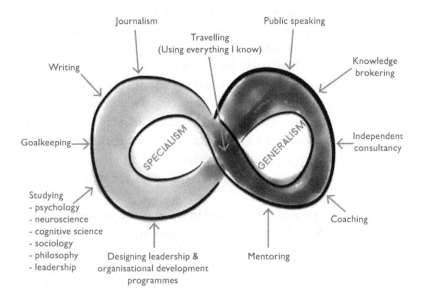

[*Figure 3.2. Kenneth's loop*]

In life, there is one choice in particular that has challenged me. It relates to the fine balance between commitment and independence. In most matters, I have held a flexible position like a tenant with a short-term lease. *No strings attached* has been my mantra. Freedom to think, learn, do and be is one of my most dominant values. Being an independent allows me to be in charge of my own destiny and work on projects that I am passionate about. One day I operate as a writer, speaker or adviser, the next as a designer and facilitator of leadership development programmes. It is a vulnerable position filled with ambivalence and self-doubt. As an independent, I do not have the luxury of being invited in or offered opportunities because I carry a title or represent a large organisation. I have to be comfortable with making my own path and standing alone, exposed and vulnerable.

Most of the accomplishments I am proud of have involved moving outside my comfort zone. When my consultancy activities found a natural level, I started playing with the idea of living somewhere else and learning a new language. Once again I became a wanderer in search of paths to other worlds. Ernest Hemingway called Paris a *moveable feast*, a state of being that becomes a part of you if you are lucky enough to have lived there in your youth. I internalised these words when I moved to Paris. Anyone who has lived in the city has a favourite story to tell. Mine is one of shapeshifting. In the morning I worked with clients and in the afternoon I transformed into an urban explorer, a flâneur in search of the Parisian soul. There was nothing I enjoyed more than wandering on foot through the backstreets of Paris. I took to heart that a good traveller has no fixed plans and is not intent on arriving. When roaming the streets, I would set out with a beginning and a vague end in mind, leaving options open to drift and respond to emerging encounters. When you walk aimlessly, you follow a trail that eventually leads to yourself. Paris managed to make my heart beat faster, exhaust me and renew me. But it also grounded me when I met my future wife, Louise, in front of

The Thinker in the garden of Musée Rodin. *Journeys end in lovers meeting*, as William Shakespeare states in *Twelfth Night*.

Somehow I have always known that my life would be lived in cycles. This challenges me to constantly adapt and adjust my view of the world and my role in it. It prompts frequent reflection and constant learning. Personal knowledge mastery has become essential to how I accomplish this. Digital technologies and social networks have enabled me to listen louder and be part of a larger conversation; to expand my understanding of the world. The ability to seek, sense and share information has assisted me in becoming a self-directed, autonomous learner.

In recent years, I have combined investigative research into neuroscience, philosophy, history, cognitive science, psychology and sociology. This has supplemented and enhanced my work on coaching and mentoring leaders. The insights I have gained from both research and practice have led me to question the leadership industry and its underlying dogma. It made me realise that there was something bigger in play, resulting in major cultural and societal shifts. This required a new approach to both leadership and education, with an emphasis on systemic change, new skills, inclusive behaviours and flexible mindsets. As a journalist, I was trained to be a transmitter of other people's opinions, evaluations and judgements. It has been an interesting challenge to learn, through a trial-and-error approach, how to voice personal ideas and thoughts in public as a writer and speaker.

For me, being a neo-generalist has roots in three principles: daring, caring and sharing. Dare to think beyond the boundaries of the known, to go in new directions. Care about the way you work, treat other people and generate a living. Share to inspire others, create real value and benefit the common good. In Africa there is a saying: *If you want to go fast, go alone. If you want to go far, go together.* Social learning through friendships and connections with wise people has played an important role in my formation. As I progress in my role as a neo-generalist, I know that inter-sections are a fertile ground for learning and growth and that I need to balance my need for independence with finding allies, and forming partnerships that can help me go further.

WANDERING TOGETHER

> *What hidden telegraphies of dreams united*
> *them now, beneath the impacted soil?*
> Adrian Mathews, *The Hat of Victor Noir*

It was love of the written word that first brought Kenneth and Richard together. Mutual appreciation of online articles and curated content led to connection on social platforms. Conversations via Twitter and Skype, exploration of numerous shared interests, resulted in a deeper bond. Attendance at a digital enterprise conference in Paris cemented the friendship. Within months we had determined to write a book together, with poly-mathic generalism the loose area of focus. The key moment, how-ever, was not the conference itself but our truancy from it. The Père Lachaise cemetery was near to the venue; too tempting an attraction to ignore.

Père Lachaise is like a salon for the dead spread out across sev-eral acres. Nobles nestle alongside politicians, academics, scien-tists, artists, poets, composers and musicians. Molière, Frédéric Chopin, Georges Méliès, Oscar Wilde, Victor Noir, Amedeo Modigliani, Edith Piaf, Jean-Dominique Bauby and Jim Morrison, to name but a few. With a little imagination, a visitor can hear polyphonic voices below the ground, like the dead townspeople of

Juan Rulfo's *Pedro Páramo*, exchanging ideas, proposing intriguing collaborations.

As we wandered along the tranquil, tree-lined avenues, passing one tombstone after another, our conversation jumped in many different directions. Names of the dead unearthed new stories, personal passions, deep knowledge. In a short time, we grew to understand one another better. We left the cemetery enriched by the experience. As we returned to the more prosaic proceedings of the business conference, we both wondered how together we could make a difference.

WHAT'S PAST IS PROLOGUE

Nothing changed, except the point of view –
which changed everything.
Nick Sousanis, *Unflattening*

In the next section of the book, we will encounter an array of boundary-crossing people who continuously jump back and forth across the infinite loop of the specialist–generalist continuum. These are researchers, consultants, entrepreneurs, environmentalists, teachers, investors, scientists, artists, sports coaches, military personnel. They come from many different countries, embody a range of cultural heritages, and span the age spectrum from the mid-twenties to the mid-eighties. Their very diversity defies the ease of categorisation that is sought in a simplified world. They accept ambiguity. Conversations with them are educational in both directions. Such people are both interested and interesting. They share their own knowledge while remaining open and receptive to new ideas and challenges to their thinking.

These men and women tell stories that both amplify and diverge from those we have shared in this chapter. But in their own way their stories also illustrate the breadth of generalism and the depth of specialism sketched out within the infinite loop. Their stories also shine a light on the different behaviours and characteristics that typify neo-generalism, from curiosity and frequency hopping to learning agility and self-realisation, from wandering and bridge-building to empathic reframing and knowledge brokerage, from horizon scanning and navigating to leadership and playmaking.

What has been read to date, then, serves as a prologue to these further explorations.

PART

4.
WHITE NOISE

Everything is concealed in symbolism, hidden by veils of mystery and layers of cultural material. But it is psychic data, absolutely. The large doors slide open, they close unbidden. Energy waves, incident radiation. All the letters and numbers are here, all the colors of the spectrum, all the voices and sounds, all the code words and ceremonial phrases. It is just a question of deciphering, rearranging, peeling off the layers of unspeakability.

Don DeLillo, *White Noise*

Knowledge comes with death's release, sang David Bowie on 'Quicksand'. Reverberations from the collision of two black holes a billion light years away washed up on Earth's shores in September 2015 to illustrate the point. The announcement on 11 February 2016 that scientists working at Laser Interferometer Gravitational-Wave Observatory (LIGO) had detected gravitational waves emanating from the collision anticipated a remapping of our knowledge horizons. The discovery validated a theory espoused by Albert Einstein a century before. With light and radio waves, astronomers had been able to extend our understanding of stars, galaxies and the expansion of the universe. With gravitational waves there is now the prospect of peering further back into spacetime, making sense of what lies in the darkness, journeying back to the singularity of the big bang itself.

Marcelo Gleiser observes in *The Island of Knowledge* that the acquisition of knowledge exposes us to our ignorance, motivating us to ask more questions. We acquire knowledge regarding a particular subject, following a breadcrumb trail of curiosity that forever leads to the boundaries of the unknown. With scientific progress the boundaries shift often as we receive answers to those questions. We are always in an ambiguous beta state, fluctuating between knowledge and not knowing. As with the LIGO researchers, we have to use sensors, trying to tune in to the right frequencies in order to receive data to process, information to assist our sense-making. In Don DeLillo's novel *White Noise*, the narrator describes the roar of sound, the bombardment of the senses, hidden meaning just beyond reach. The challenge is to learn how to listen, see, filter, sense, in order to gain some form of understanding, however transitory. The waves of light, radiation and gravity are continuums, the journeys along which will lead us to insight.

Life on the neo-generalist spectrum can be like spinning the dial on an old-fashioned FM radio. Change the channel, jump across the continuum, switch the discipline, frequency hop from deep specialism to polymathic generalism. Between the pre-programmed stations, the nodes on the network, there is white noise. But fine-tuning can pick up weak signals, hidden broadcasts, channels through which to emit our own sound. Discernment, selection and amplification are necessary. The days of the single RKO beacon atop the globe are long behind us. Today, everyone is a potential broadcaster, a mobile generator of noise, emitting different interpretations of the world around us, their respective signals clashing and interfering with one another. The danger, as Buckminster Fuller articulates it in *Synergetics*, is that to spend too long in a specialist realm is to restrict wide-band tuning. This in turn precludes discovery of generalised principles.

In the domain of theoretical physics, the concept of wave–particle duality has been explained in terms of a tale about six blind men and an elephant. As Werner Heisenberg explains in *Physics and Philosophy*, what we observe is not nature itself but a version of nature exposed to our own questioning. There is a disjuncture between perception and reality. 'The Blind Men and the Elephant' is a well-known parable that originated in the Indian subcontinent. Explored from a variety of religious and philosophical perspectives, it has been distilled into verse by John Godfrey Saxe: *It was six men of Indostan / To learning much inclined, / Who went to see the Elephant / (Though all of them were blind), / That each by observation / Might satisfy his mind.* The blind men make use of the sense of touch to gain an understanding of what an elephant is. The first touches the elephant's sturdy flank, the second a tusk, the third its trunk, the fourth a knee, the fifth an ear, the sixth its tail. All gain distinct impressions.

Each of the blind men alights on a different frequency, making analogies with knowledge already in their possession, and as a consequence completely misinterpret the animal they encounter. Their tuning has been constrained. One detects a wall, another a spear, the others respectively a snake, a tree, a fan and a rope. Each demonstrates the convictions of the hedgehog, adamant that they have the one right answer. The parable is the subject of analysis in Steve Hardy's *The Creative Generalist* manifesto, and was suggested to us by David Hain who is a business consultant specialising in people and change. Drawing on his own interests in Buddhism and quantum theory, David argues that it is the neo-generalist, in their capacity of facilitator and co-creator, who helps synthesise these different perspectives.

The neo-generalist pulls together the fragments, assembles the puzzle pieces, to establish the big picture. By inhabiting spaces in between different knowledge domains, they are capable of casting a wide net over multiple topics. They help others achieve clarity. In *Zen and the Art of Motorcycle Maintenance*, Robert Pirsig's narrator observes, 'We're living in topsy-turvy times, and I think that what caused the topsy-turvy feeling is inadequacy of old forms of thought to deal with new experiences.' The neo-generalist is receptive to new ways of thinking, combining them with established philosophies, tweaking and remixing. They are a source of oxygen for insiders, bridging to people and ideas from outside established spheres of practice and organisation. They are among the few people who see the whole picture, the ones who step out of the frame. Indeed, they are constantly reframing, searching for another view, hunting for what is next.

The notion of reframing has been a constant factor in Prasad Kaipa's life as he has travelled across the specialist–generalist continuum. Prasad grew up in India, where he attained a PhD in Physics from the Indian Institute of Technology, Madras. He opted to pursue an academic career in the USA, initially working as a researcher and lecturer at the University of Utah, specialising in the effects of nuclear radiation. Prasad became an early adopter of personal computing in the 1980s, and was soon involved in software testing and writing articles for prominent magazines. He eventually joined Apple Computers, as it was then known, where he worked alongside graphics designer Bill Atkinson on a project that explored how people learn, lead, collaborate, think and create. As part of the project, the team interviewed more than 200 Nobel laureates, authors, musicians, educators, spiritual leaders and sports people.

The experience helped Prasad realise that what others might view as white noise, laden with information, seemingly at the point of overwhelming them, he understood as a space filled with infinite possibilities and opportunities. Imagination, focus and fine-tuning allow us to identify possibilities to pursue. Our passions, interests and excitement enable us to translate these possibilities into opportunities. Mahatma Gandhi, for example, progressed from the possibility of pursuing civil rights interests in South Africa to fulfilling a leadership opportunity in India. His political views and ethics developed as a result of his experiences in his South African legal practice. They served as a foundation for everything that was to follow upon returning to his homeland and becoming involved in the struggle for Indian independence.

It is the interplay between values and beliefs, moods and assumptions, perspectives and attitudes, that influence how we determine what is worth pursuing in life. For Prasad, corporate life as an employee was not his end goal. In 1990, he left Apple University, where he was involved in the company's leadership development programme, to become an independent adviser and consultant to senior executives. Since then, he has co-founded an IT company in Silicon Valley, sat on several boards, and taught executive courses in leadership, mindset change and innovation in some of the leading business schools in the world. His diversity of experience informs his numerous publications.

Among these is the book *From Smart to Wise: Acting and Leading with Wisdom*, which Prasad co-authored with Navi Radjou.

The authors recognise that it is inevitable that many people will find themselves in a white noise environment, confronted by the increased complexity, diversity and ambiguity that characterises modern society. Prasad and Navi believe that the cultivation of wisdom offers a way to address what can initially appear disconcerting. At the heart of wisdom, they argue, is noble purpose; a North Star that helps us to orient ourselves and navigate in times of change. In some respects, their ideas echo those of Aristotle in *The Politics*, in which he distinguishes between surviving and living. Surviving means defying death by fulfilling our physical needs and staying out of harm's way. Living, on the other hand, focuses on the study of philosophy and ethics, with the aspiration to grow and thrive.

Aristotle created a masterclass for leaders on Cyprus in the fourth century BCE. The intention was to encourage each leader to concentrate on what was essential in their lives, to examine their values and ethics. For Aristotle, practical wisdom and personal excellence were central to a good life, but the principal aspiration was to achieve *eudaimonia*, a state of human flourishing. *Protreptic*, which captures the idea of turning a person towards their own essence, is the art of stewarding others in pursuit of such a good life. This is not a selfish exercise. It requires understanding how we can reach our full potential while taking the greater community into account. It is the willingness to reframe perspectives and challenge perceptions at the core of our value system. It prevents us from living in ignorance, leading to what Socrates referred to as 'the examined life'. In recent years, philosopher Ole Fogh Kirkeby has been an advocate of the protreptic dialogue as a professor at Copenhagen Business School in Denmark. He believes this dialogue is key to unlocking personal reflection and learning. The neo-generalist is uniquely positioned to serve as a steward of these conversations. They are always searching, way-finding, reflecting, becoming. Their own experience enables them to guide others.

When Kenneth, one of this book's authors, travelled to India to establish himself as a freelance foreign correspondent, he experienced the ambiguity that comes from being enveloped by white noise. His quest for meaning and purpose led him to search for new channels to tune into outside his familiar milieu. He had opted out of a steady job that conflicted with his values. Now he was embedded in a new cultural context, one that was a cause both for concern and excitement. In a letter that he sent to his parents on his thirtieth birthday, Kenneth expressed how growing up with multiple interests had posed a constant challenge, opening up a wide range of options to explore and choose from. Finding the right channel had been a journey in which balance was continually lost and recovered. It was an inescapable path, a possible route he could not ignore. 'I simply had to go in a new direction,' he wrote. 'Where the road takes me is unknown but my mind is at peace knowing that I have always picked up a signal when it was needed.'

Change is confusing and unsettling. In modern life, a lack of stability, a lack of equilibrium, has become the norm rather than the exception. Society's shifting tectonic plates pose a challenge. The individual lives in a state of continually becoming. Constant motion is necessary to achieve balance and progression. Simone de Beauvoir touched on this in *The Ethics of Ambiguity*, observing that: 'life is occupied in both perpetuating itself and surpassing itself; if all it does is maintain itself, then living is only not dying'. When our worldview and what we hold to be true is challenged, we experience a sense of disorientation, a culture shock. In Buddhism, the term *dukkha* describes this state of being. Dukkha is the pain we experience when we cannot figure out how to let go of what no longer exists. It is usually translated into English as *suffering* but it also means *temporary*, *limited* and *imperfect*.

Matthew McConaughey won an Oscar for his performance as lead actor in *Dallas Buyers Club* in 2014. In his acceptance speech, he mentioned three things that he finds essential on a daily basis: something to *chase*, something to *look forward to* and something to *look up to*. These drivers also sustain people when they find themselves swamped by white noise. The feeling that there is no arrival, that we never reach a final destination, can be a source of inspiration. Joy and excitement come from following personal passions and being with people we respect, love and from whom we learn. Looking up to something means having a guiding light that provides inner meaning, a purpose that goes beyond ourselves. This is not to suggest that life's journey is without its difficulties. Swiss psychiatrist and psychotherapist Carl Jung believed that we all have a shadow side, an inner drive that invites discovery, drawing us on despite the risk. Left unattended, the darker and denser it becomes. Personal growth involves shining light on to our shadow self. There we find disorientation, pain and loss. It is from our own vulnerability that we learn and grow the most. This is the essence of being accountable, taking ownership of all aspects of our lives, both light and dark.

Anne McCrossan argues that the current era of accelerated transformation is a pivotal moment in human existence. It is one of deep, existential enquiry, necessitating that we carve out space for reflection and identify the tools and resources that will enable us to achieve understanding. Anne has been making waves and challenging the establishment since her youth. She rejected a scholarship at Cambridge University, piquing the interest of fifteen different London advertising agencies as a result of her actions. Anne was determined not to just take what was being offered to her. If someone was suggesting North, she was looking to the East, West and South as well. She often found herself at the cutting edge as she developed expertise in identity and digital design.

Anne has worked with many of the world's leading brands, including Apple, which she helped launch in the UK. She was also a founder member of Seth Godin's Tribes project. In 2008,

Anne founded Visceral Business, which takes a people-first approach to digital strategy and organisation. Through her agency and consultancy work, Anne has been exposed to a diversity of different industries, which range from the pharmaceutical to the technological, from government to children's games. Constantly, she submerges herself in different learning contexts, identifying what interests her, seeking to learn from those that she acknowledges as leading figures in their respective fields.

Russian psychologist Lev Vygotsky has inspired generations of psychologists and teachers to reconceive how we learn. He was one of the first to recognise humans as cultural beings, highlighting how learning is social, how we evolve in relation to the culture we live in. Vygotsky argues that we need a 'more knowledgeable other' to help guide us through the complexities of learning. He speaks of the 'zone of proximal development', by which he means the difference between what a learner can achieve with and without assistance from others. The inclusion of other people is an approach to learning that suits Anne well, as she expands her knowledge and experience, fosters communities and practises her own craft skills as a potter. Anne is a kinaesthetic learner. Working and studying alongside others, she claims, makes her even better. She accepts that none of us can claim to have the absolute truth of a situation. What we have to do is make the most of the partial knowledge that every one of us has, combining what we know, learning from one another.

Not long before Anne's father died, he paid a visit to her house. It was in a chaotic state for which Anne apologised. His warm and considerate response was that it was because Anne was interested in too many things. Anne felt that it was as if he had waited thirty years to tell her this, finally sharing his insight about her open and eclectic character. Anne has always been interested in the connection between things and not just in the things themselves. In the very diversity of what she does and the interests she pursues, crossing borders between multiple disciplines, discovering a sense of belonging in both the digital and analogue domains, demonstrating a passionate enthusiasm for people and their ideas, Anne epitomises what it is to be a neo-generalist.

Surrounded by the white noise of the modern world, whether through her work, her community building or her craft activities, Anne finds the capacity to tune in to different frequencies, deriving sense from chaos. In the following chapters, as we explore learning and education, identity and shapeshifting, multidisciplinarity, community, empathy, change agency, sense-making, storytelling, leadership and legacy, we will encounter many other people who are similarly adept at making their way through many worlds. They switch channels as the context shifts, frequency hopping, constantly fine-tuning their sensors and skills.

5.
PICARESQUE
TALES

*I can give you neither gold nor silver,
but I will supply you with devices
that will help you survive.*

Anonymous, *Lazarillo de Tormes*

In Donna Tartt's novel *The Goldfinch*, protagonist Theo Decker enters an extended period of apprenticeship following his mother's death. From the surrogate father figure Hobie, Theo acquires the craft of furniture restoration; from his school friend Boris, he receives an education in criminality and transgression. One world infects the other via Theo's own agency. *The Goldfinch* sketches out a journey of youthful learning and an exploration of life in the margins. As such, it belongs in part to the tradition of the coming-of-age *Bildungsroman*, in part to that of the picaresque novel. The latter can be traced back to the anonymous publication in Spain of *Lazarillo de Tormes* in the middle of the sixteenth century. In this short, controversial work, the eponymous anti-hero attaches himself to numerous masters living on the edge, giving expression to the mischievous side of the trickster, learning the distinction between perception and reality. Lázaro's self-centred immersion in the craft of deception satirises the traditional path from apprenticeship to mastery. Theo's own experience is more complicated. He lives in many worlds, is more overtly aware of his hybrid existence, his travels on the continuum.

The apprentice's journey has a deep heritage. The original Tour de France, established long before the invention of the bicycle, was followed by apprentice masons, carpenters and others who undertook a journey lasting several years around the region of the Massif Central. According to Graham Robb, in his *The Discovery of France*, these wandering craftsmen would visit up to 151 different towns and villages, spending weeks in each, learning the local techniques for their chosen discipline through both observation and practice, before moving on to the next. During the tour, the apprentice would be inducted into their respective guild. A similar tradition existed in northern European countries like Germany and Denmark. In medieval times, guilds in these regions were an important part of city and town life. They enforced an exclusionary economy that protected the craftsmen and their expertise against outside competition and poor workmanship. Guilds were associations of specialists. To progress in rank, one had to pass through three stages, experiencing the respective roles of apprentice, journeyman and master.

Each guild kept track of the number of masters in towns and ensured that everyone within the profession was properly trained. The journeyman first had to produce a masterpiece as evidence of his craftsmanship, presenting it to the guild before he could be accepted as a member and earn the right to open a workshop. The journey was a continuation of their apprenticeship, representing an opportunity for craftsmen to acquire new perspectives, skills and knowledge in their field of expertise. The length of the journey varied with the craft and served as preparation for mastery. For example, craftsmen such as carpenters, masons, blacksmiths and painters journeyed for three years and a day. A journeyman was expected to be unmarried, childless and debt-free to ensure that the trip was not undertaken as an escape from social obligations. While wandering from one town to another, the journeyman carried only a sleeping bag, a curled hiking stick and a leather backpack of clothes and tools. To distinguish themselves from tramps, who sought to exploit the system, they wore a black hat with a broad brim which symbolised a free man. A tie revealed their artisanal association and a pin indicated which guild they belonged to. The uniform was completed by a gold earring the value of which could cover the cost of their funeral if they were to die during the journey. The journeyman was only allowed to stay in any one place for a period of six months, never venturing closer than fifty kilometres to their hometown.

A journeyman depended on their specialist skills to sustain a living. But knowledge of a craft was not enough to survive in uncharted territory for three years. They constantly had to adapt to different techniques, unfamiliar languages and opposing perspectives regarding their craft. Changing situations offered opportunities to learn and combine new concepts with old practices.

From a social perspective, the journeyman was a transmitter of cultural values and knowledge, ensuring a constant renewal and development of craft traditions and designs. They might have learned a special technique from one project that could later be applied elsewhere, in a different town or a country where it was unknown. Journeymen were both students and teachers. They learned by doing and showing, challenging mental models through their actions. Time spent wandering was useful for reflection and gave the journeyman an opportunity to integrate lessons from their experiences. At the start of their travels, such craftsmen would only carry a small, fixed sum of money. They were expected to return with the same amount in their pocket. The journey was to be undertaken for the expansion of knowledge, cultural awareness and experience, not the accumulation or squandering of wealth. There is much that modern society can learn from the journeyman concept.

Ting Kelly is a modern journeywoman. Born in San Francisco to a Taiwanese mother and an American father, she grew up exposed to a wide range of disciplines including calligraphy, dancing, mathematics and languages in a Chinese-American school. Influenced by her father's maker spirit, she learned how to build toys and carry out science experiments at home. Ting completed studies in architecture and woodwork at Lick-Wilmerding High School, before earning a degree in International Relations and Affairs from the University of British Columbia in Vancouver. By the age of twenty, she had already completed six different internships. A preference for making things by hand, combined with a deep understanding of form, composition, colours and shapes has enabled Ting to apply herself in various disciplines as a designer, curator and community builder. Her first job after graduation was in a communications firm. She designed a curriculum for leadership development and led a team that was responsible for building relationships with Silicon Valley start-ups and incubators. However, Ting felt underutilised and struggled with being labelled as a marketeer.

In 2013, Ting set out on a learning journey with her partner Bjorn Cooley to map, catalogue and connect the leaders of twelve innovation ecosystems in Asia. During their travels, they met with 150 entrepreneurs, makers and hackers over the course of four months. The journey was self-funded. While on the road, Ting and Bjorn continued to run their newly-established company Doorstep Studios, which specialises in brand and strategy consulting for social enterprises, foundations, non-profits and start-ups. Three times a week they blogged about their encounters, showcasing the ideas that emerged from the conversations. The idea for the Asian learning journey took root when Ting and Bjorn had relocated to Detroit a few months earlier to explore and document a burning question: *What is next?* Areas of transitions have always interested Ting. In Detroit, she used an anthropological approach to profile how makers were building entrepreneurial spaces in a fractured community. The attempt to renew and establish greater resilience in a run-down area opened Ting's eyes to a new world. It was through conversation that she learned that the creative culture, symbolised by places like New York and the Bay Area, was not exclusive to those locations. Rather, it was part of a growing global movement that was on the rise in places as diverse as Detroit and Beijing.

As an extrovert, Ting prefers to learn with and from others. Digital technologies mostly serve as a structural layer to gather information, facilitate conversations and coordinate in-person meet-ups. Much like the medieval journeyman, she uses a playful combination of cultural immersion and apprenticeship to accelerate and transmit her learning. Her commitment to bridging cultures and generations is manifested through her work for the Long Now Foundation where she has been a member since she was fourteen years of age. Ting's involvement in the foundation, which aims to provide a counterpoint to today's faster/cheaper mindset, offers her an opportunity to engage with like-spirited people who seek to promote slower/better thinking and devise creative, long-term solutions to some of the pressing challenges in our society. Ting's story exemplifies the importance of role models in our formative years. From her father, Kevin Kelly, Ting developed a love of learning. Kevin, the co-founder of *Wired* magazine, nurtured in her the confidence to try new things, to generalise and become a self-educator. Intriguingly, though, it was her mother, biochemist Gia-Miin Fuh, who taught her the value of specialisation, of focusing on the completion of projects of greatest importance to her. Ting learned from role models who gravitate towards different positions on the specialist–generalist continuum.

Lucian Tarnowski is someone who also absorbs learning from travelling and inspirational role models. He was born into a prominent, aristocratic family with deep cultural roots in both Poland and the UK. Lucian's father, Arthur Tarnowski, narrowly escaped death after Poland fell under the Soviet regime in the aftermath of World War II. In the early 1950s, Arthur started backpacking around the world at a time when it was a largely unknown phenomenon. During a trip to Bali, in his late twenties, he contracted polio, which left him paralysed from the waist down, wheelchair-bound for the rest of his life. Despite his disability, he continued to travel. In 1964, Arthur set out on a 100,000-mile expedition to assess the situation of physically-handicapped people and explore local vocational education and rehabilitation solutions.

It was during this journey, while at the Anandwan ashram in India, that Arthur met his best friend, lifelong mentor and adopted father Baba Amte. Baba was a protégé of Gandhi, and became known as one of the greatest social workers and activists in India. The friendship inspired Lucian's father to establish a charity, Take Heart, that provides aid to and supports the rehabilitation of the physically-handicapped people of rural India. Love of the other became a central theme in Arthur Tarnowski's life. Having lived through the horrors of World War II, he saw education and vocational training as a way to prevent future wars and for the handicapped to regain their sense of dignity and self-worth. In India, the charity's practical education projects give people the skills needed to gain employment or start a company which prevents them from living as beggars.

Mark Twain is alleged to have said, 'The two most important days in your life are the day you are born and the day you find out why.' Lucian's purpose is intrinsically linked to his father's experiences and learning. When Lucian and his brother Sebastian were born, their father was already in his fifties. Much of his time was dedicated to his children's learning. Arthur introduced the boys to different cultures as they accompanied him on journeys abroad. For Lucian, it became a natural thing to switch perspective and decode foreign situations. Travelling and meeting people in their local environment instilled in him a love of the other and a sense of connection with his roots. Early on in life, Lucian knew he had to strive to accomplish something beyond his own personal interests. He refers to it as 'humble audacity'. The skills he brings on this journey, already spanning more than sixty countries, is natural curiosity and a deep desire to learn. As someone with dyslexia, Lucian learns best in conversation. His large personal network serves as a feeding ground for fresh ideas and an accelerator of learning.

When Lucian graduated from the University of Edinburgh with a master's degree in Comparative Religion, he had already taken on responsibility for running the family charity. He did so on the condition that everyone previously involved in the management of the foundation retired. Lucian saw new possibilities in using technology to further advance the charity's impact. Discouraged by the formal education system's inability to keep up with the exponential pace of change in society, Lucian took his father's advice to heart: if you want to change the system, go around it. By organising fundraising events, while still at university, Lucian raised enough money to build an English language and IT school in India that specialises in training blind students. The IT skills that they acquire provide them with a job for life. A second project followed where the charity established a hostel that is home to 120 blind and handicapped girls while they study at the school.

Typical of a neo-generalist, Lucian has a keen eye for making connections between ideas and people. In 2007, on his 89th birthday, Nelson Mandela founded The Elders with the help of Graça Machel and Desmond Tutu. The idea was conceived in a conversation between the entrepreneur Richard Branson and the musician Peter Gabriel. Mandela brought together ten Elders – independent, progressive leaders committed to using their collective experience and influence to help tackle some of the most pressing problems facing the world, from climate change to violent conflict. Lucian reached out to one of its members, Ela Bhatt, to outline his vision. He suggested that a similar group, The Youngers, should be established to allow for an inter-generational dialogue. The idea was not implemented but it brought Lucian into contact with Kate Robertson, co-founder of One Young World. The organisation, created in 2009, assembles young leaders from all parts of the world to discuss and work on similar grand-scale problems. Lucian joined the team as a delegate and was subsequently included in the World Economic Forum's programme for young global leaders.

Lucian was experiencing key life lessons at a young age; something that went beyond education, shaping and informing the man he was to become. It is a phenomenon that has a deep cultural heritage, inspired by philosophers and captured in art. In the late eighteenth century, for example, the polymathic Goethe wrote what is now celebrated as the first *Bildungsroman*, *Wilhelm Meister's Apprenticeship*. In the novel and its sequel, *Wilhelm Meister's Journeyman Years*, the reader follows Wilhelm as he searches for answers to life's big questions and undergoes a personal transformation. The story centres on his attempt to resist all pigeonholing and escape what he views as the empty life of a bourgeois businessman.

Goethe's Meister novels unite two literary genres. The confessional novel, with its focus on individual development, and the picaresque tale, where the environment and surroundings change. One covers the inner, psychological journey, the other the outer, physical one. To develop as humans, we need both introspection and outrospection. Nothing evolves in a vacuum. During his apprenticeship, Wilhelm undertakes a personal project to learn a craft. Throughout his journeyman years, however, he pursues an outwardly-focused journey in order to apply himself in society. It is in the intersection between the self and the world that he achieves his full potential as a human being. Only by being willing to challenge his perception of reality, itself shaped by his previous experiences, does he develop his ability to live a rich and fulfilling life with others.

It was the mystical theologian Meister Eckhart who first placed *Bildung* in a pedagogical context in the thirteenth century. The German word *Bildung* also exists in Scandinavian countries but it cannot be translated easily into English. It refers to the shaping of a human individual's personality, behaviour and moral attitude through their upbringing, environment and education. Neither *education* nor *formation* suffice to cover the comprehensive and complex meaning of the word. *Bildung* is a much broader concept, encompassing knowledge, judgement, a broad cultural and political orientation, an understanding of science and technology, and a cultivation of the fine arts. *Bildung* traces its roots to the Judaeo-Christian belief that humans should carry an image of God in their hearts and strive to cultivate their talents according to it. Meister Eckhart's notion of *Bildung*, then, originates in the terms *imago* and *forma*, in the sense intended in the Latin version of St Paul's second letter to the Corinthians (3:18): *in eandem imaginem transformamur* (are transformed into the same image).

A more rounded concept of *Bildung* materialised in the eighteenth century with the Enlightenment as an influential catalyst.

Having been associated with the Christian faith, *Bildung* then developed into a humanistic philosophy with the liberated individual as the focal point. German thinkers such as Winckelmann, Herder, Hölderlin, Goethe, Schiller and Hegel considered the time of the Ancient Greeks as the period in which humanity had reached its highest stage of expression and formation. They were inspired by *paideia*, the Greek idea of perfection and excellence, and by the Roman philosopher Cicero's later concept of *humanitas*. They believed that an individual needed to possess certain virtues in order to be suitable both for public service and a fulfilling private life. As such, the emergence of *Bildung* was a counter-reaction to the formation of the one-sided man.

The philosopher Wilhelm von Humboldt defined *Bildung* as 'the highest and most balanced development of man'. For Humboldt, who was among the founders of the University of Berlin, the *gebildete* person was someone who had cultivated and developed all of their abilities in an equal manner, rather than specialising in a narrow field. Mastery of language was important. It mediated people and their environment, serving as an entry ticket to new territories and fields of interest. By acquiring wide and in-depth knowledge, the individual becomes morally and spiritually educated, as well as a useful citizen. The core principle in *Bildung* is that humans actively take responsibility for developing themselves, their community and the world they are part of. Uniting the three spheres in mutual interplay requires a holistic perspective taking *we* into consideration and not just focusing on *me*. The understanding and appreciation of interdependence enables individuals to reach their potential and opens the door to the peaceful coexistence of humanity. Without empathy, benevolence and generosity one cannot become a *gebildete* person.

Formal education is something that you end with an exam, but *Bildung* is never finished. A cultivated life provides a sense of orientation and builds bridges between our domains of knowledge and experiences. Theory is of little value in and of itself. Only through action and reflection can we gain a deeper understanding of its usefulness. In creative moments, when dots are connected, innovative ideas are born. Cognition, creative insight and emotional intelligence are prerequisites for critical thinking. Our capacity to solve complex problems and make wise decisions rely on having something to attach new knowledge and experiences to. It implies that we humans have a broad horizon and are capable of evaluating future opportunities and threats in the light of past and present events. *Bildung* requires that we meet the world with curiosity and wonder. It goes beyond thinking and learning, embracing how we act and live; how we adjust our approach in context. It is both a lifelong challenge and opportunity from which we can derive meaning and discover purpose.

The cultures in which we find ourselves shape and condition us, but they are in turn influenced by us. *Bildung* is a dynamic concept that evolves over time. What Goethe, Humboldt and their contemporaries perceived as *Bildung* is different again today. Conceptually, it has shifted as our understanding of what it means to be human has changed. To orientate ourselves in the modern world, we must take accelerating social, technological and scientific advancements into account. Globalisation, artificial intelligence, robotics, biotechnology, big data, 3D printing, quantum computing, climate change and a growing world population are just some of the interconnected issues that we face as a species. We have to adapt, challenging how we learn, how we put that into practice and, at a more fundamental level, our very way of life. In times of transition, *Bildung* will be of central importance just as it was during the Enlightenment.

In many respects, we find ourselves at the edge of the unknown. According to the US Department of Labor, for example, nearly two-thirds of children who attend primary school today will work in jobs that have not yet been invented. Knowledge itself is becoming increasingly ephemeral, with the average life-span from acquisition to obsolescence calculated at approximately five years. Learning is at the core of any personal or organisational transformation. As we progress into unfamiliar territory, we will need to become more adept at rapid, relevant and autonomous learning. There is no other way we can address the wicked problems facing us. A slide of the thumb across a mobile phone, a few quick keystrokes on a personal computer, can connect us to new worlds. We can study any subject via online courses, videos, blogs, podcasts, webinars and books. We can engage any time and anywhere. The possibilities of undertaking self-education, of becoming autonomous, self-directed learners has never been greater at any other time in history. So crucial is the need to be adaptive and responsive, that futurist and philosopher Alvin Toffler believes that the illiterate of the current century will be those who cannot modify their learning in response to change.

Information technologies have affected how we live, work and learn. The internet has established new ways of communicating with other people, sharing knowledge, forming perspectives and questioning things. It has enabled access to an overwhelming volume of information, connecting us to people across cultures in online communities and networks. Asmelash Zeferu epitomises this better than most people. His childhood dream was to become a pilot. After having been rejected by the Ethiopian Airlines Aviation Academy, he decided to build his own aeroplane. The fact that Zeferu had never flown before mattered little to him. Over a period of ten years, he studied YouTube tutorials and underwent three different apprenticeships, equipping himself with the skills to build and fly the aircraft. In a parallel and equally remarkable learning journey, Kenyan Julius Yego won gold medal in javelin at the 2015 World Athletics Championships having taught himself the event. Like Zeferu, he achieved this by studying YouTube videos and experimenting with technique. Both men are fuelled by passion and curiosity, as well as a willingness to learn by doing.

The digital revolution actualises the relevance of *Bildung*. In *The Question Concerning Technology*, German philosopher Martin Heidegger observed that 'the essence of technology is by no means anything technological'. It is instead about human beings. The self-directed learner must develop his or her own personal framework for acquiring new knowledge. Knowing how to build relationships, seek information, make sense of observations and share ideas with others through an intelligent use of technology is imperative. Personal knowledge mastery, a term coined by business and learning consultant Harold Jarche, is essentially a lifelong learning strategy, bridging both digital and analogue worlds, whereby individuals learn how to learn. The continuous process of seeking, sensing-making and sharing is a way to take control of our personal development. Heidegger warned that technology could potentially bring about our decline by constricting our experience of things as they are. Digital literacy is more than just understanding how to use new technologies. It is also the ability to understand *why* and *how* we use it and for what purposes. Questioning how technology influences our behaviour, values and the way we see ourselves and the world are equally important. The will to mastery becomes all the more urgent the more technology threatens to slip from human control.

The road to such mastery is not always straightforward as many neo-generalist stories illustrate. Dolly Garland's home is in three countries on three different continents. She grew up in India, moved to the USA at the age of fifteen, and now lives in the UK. Having been exposed to the formal educational system in three countries, she playfully refers to herself as a Dolly Mixture. Growing up, she attended both private and public schools, going on to attain a degree in Finance and Economics, which she followed with a master's in English Literature. Her careful cultivation of learning defies the linear constraints of institutionalised education. It is driven by a natural curiosity. While enjoying her time spent in academia, she believes self-education is much more powerful. A 2012 blog post on her site *Kaizen Journaling* outlines a personal ambition to become a modern-day polymath.

Inspired by historical figures like Leonardo da Vinci, Benjamin Franklin and Arthur Conan Doyle, Dolly has embarked on a very deliberate polymathic journey. Her idea is to set a goal, a direction and a purpose for lifelong learning in seven areas. Her project ranges from writing to physical activities, from learning languages to understanding human behaviour. This requires multiple specialisms that together serve her overarching objective of creating a 'Kaizen Life'. The Japanese word *kaizen* means *change for better*. It is often associated with the business management concept of continuous improvement, which has also been adopted in other domains such as sport. The purpose of education for Dolly is not primarily about the acquisition of factual knowledge or specific skills, but about learning how to be human.

Dolly's concern for learning is also reflected in her professional life. As someone who insists on questioning standards and allowing people to be unique, she has consciously carved out her own career, switching between employment by others, running workshops and counselling people on journaling, a form of self-help through writing. Dolly only takes on work that brings her joy and supports her polymathic aspirations. When she reflects back on her working life in old age, she wants to have a collection of experiences, not regrets. Ting Kelly is equally passionate about transforming the way we learn and work in the twenty-first century. She started a podcast, *Lineage*, to investigate what Western societies can learn from the East; a question she has lived with her whole life. Her podcasts are wide-ranging, covering such topics as spirituality, lifestyle, wellness, the start-up life and the creative process. As she learns out loud, Ting makes her discoveries freely available for a global audience online. Both Ting and Dolly have taken education into their own hands, translating personal insight and experience into public utility, disseminating their enthusiasm and knowledge via digital channels.

So what does the future of education look like? What is an education fit for the twenty-first century? What relevance does *Bildung* have beyond its traditional stronghold in Germany and Scandinavia? Can formal education help us address the interconnected challenges in our contemporary world, helping us advance as a society? Today, most established educational institutions are designed for consistency, control and predictability. The system they represent is largely guided by and reliant upon quantifiable outcomes, founded upon standardised testing and certification. The conveyer-belt model is a relic of the Industrial era, no longer pertinent to the knowledge worker and the digital age. The gap between what is deliverable within the system and what people need to stay relevant and thrive is widening. We are beginning to see how this approach prevents organisations from adapting to a new reality where responsiveness and rapid learning are essential.

From an early age, our educational choices lock us on to a path from which it is difficult to diverge, limiting the disciplines available to us, constraining the possibility of shapeshifting later in life. The current system does not lend itself well to the curious mind. There is little room to explore, few opportunities to jump across disciplines or draw inspiration from multiple fields. In 2014, in one example of discontent with systemic constraint, the International Student Initiative for Pluralism in Economics (ISIPE) was founded in protest against mainstream economic teaching. ISIPE is a coalition of over 80 economics student groups from more than 30 countries. In a letter to *The Guardian*, the coalition argued that economics courses are failing society when they exclude ideas from other fields of study and practice.

The establishment of ISIPE highlights that students desire new methods that can help them adapt their mindset, skills and behaviour in response to future challenges. The noble purpose of education is to help students learn how to learn, and to understand what it means to belong in society, to be a citizen and take responsibility not only for themselves but also the greater good. This requires both breadth and depth of knowledge and expertise. Yet we continue with a polemic today that can be traced back at least to the time of the Renaissance, evidenced by an artificial schism between the arts and the sciences. At the heart of Stephen Jay Gould's thesis in *The Hedgehog, the Fox, and the Magister's Pox* is a call to bridge this gap, to debunk the notion of an incompatibility between these two great fields of human knowledge. It is why the current advocacy of science, technology, engineering and mathematics, the STEM subjects, by policymakers and funding bodies seems so misguided. They are essential, but so too is the study of the humanities. Indeed, an appreciation of human history, art and philosophy would teach much about what is happing in Europe and the USA right now. It is through the hybridisation of and cross-pollination between such disciplines that we will arrive at solutions for our wicked problems. It is encouraging, therefore, to see interdisciplinarity and transdisciplinarity beginning to find firm footholds in certain academic institutions.

Even as the funding of liberal arts programmes is threatened in the USA, where the promotion of STEM appears to be strengthening, in the UK new, experimental offerings are seeking a convergence of the two fields. University College London (UCL), for example, has recently established an interdisciplinary Bachelor of Arts and Sciences (BASc) degree. Students are able to work with faculty to design their own courses, in some cases accommodating a breadth of interests, in others building towards specific career objectives. It is a good example of academia enabling generalism in support of specialism, of facilitating creative connections to be made across different subjects. Carl Gombrich is UCL's programme director. He has been walking around a particular conundrum most of his adult life: 'How do you integrate

Stevie Wonder, Plato, postmodernism and politics?' Personally, he enjoys a rich cultural and intellectual heritage. His grandfather was the celebrated art historian Ernst Gombrich. Carl himself holds degrees in mathematics, physics and philosophy, and was a professional opera singer before taking up an academic post at UCL. As a teacher, leader, artist, scientist and former captain of his football team, Carl exemplifies the well-rounded character that UCL are trying to foster with their innovative approach to further education.

The evolution within the education system is not only visible within established institutions. Peter Bull is currently working on establishing the Practical University in the UK. This will offer a training programme for sixteen- to eighteen-year-olds who are not interested in pursuing traditional academic studies. The Practical University will prepare young people for life and future employment by introducing them to topics as diverse as construction, engineering, cooking, financial management, sport, coaching, the arts and voluntary work. There will be no exams. As the names suggests, the curriculum is primarily concerned with practice and action. The vision of the Practical University has parallels with that of the Soka value-creating pedagogy in Japan and the folk high school, a uniquely Danish concept supporting a broad, generalist education. The Danish schools do not award grades nor provide specialist training. As all the folk high schools are residential, they serve as micro societies, with students and staff living together, eating together and sharing the same daily routines. The schools are highly influenced by the German *Bildung* tradition and characterised by their emphasis on enlightenment, democracy, ethics and morality. Every year, approximately two per cent of Denmark's population attend the schools. They are also open for adult students during the summer months.

As we pass through different stages of our lives, the motives and needs we have for learning change. In recent years, we have seen the emergence of 'schools for life' that help students align values, life choices and social engagement. The Change School in Singapore, for example, offers multidisciplinary programmes for individuals looking to launch a business or simply find a different direction in their private life or career. The Change School's offerings vary from one-day pop-up events in different locations around the region to a twenty-one-day immersive retreat in Bali. Grace Clapham and Solonia Teodros, who founded the school in 2013, want to create a basecamp where people can both ground themselves and find direction in a complex world. Unlike formal academic institutions, it is a school you never graduate from. Such reappraisal of the educational system is reflected by decisions taken by big corporations such as Deloitte, Google, PricewaterhouseCoopers (PwC) and Ernst & Young (EY). They claim to see no evidence that success at university correlates with achievement in later life. The degree classification is no longer a passport into the workplace. Other aspects of learning and formation are being taken into consideration too.

Of course, formal education is just one of many contexts through which people learn and acquire knowledge. In complex environments, learning also results from a combination of discovery, dialogue, experience, reflection and application. Working life is increasingly one of contextual shifts, of oblique turns and sudden career changes. In order to remain relevant, both belonging to and serving the society around us, we have to be adaptive, constantly and actively learning, taking responsibility for our own education in any situation. In the speech he never delivered at the Dallas Citizens Council, John F. Kennedy observed that 'leadership and learning are indispensable to each other'. Leadership is linked to self-responsibility. As the opportunities to learn in a digital age continue to grow, it will be hard to keep up without a deep understanding of how new tools influence and shape human nature. In education and action, we continue to evolve, always becoming.

6.
PROVINCIAL PUNK

Our sense of ourselves feels constant but our identity is an ongoing performance that is changed and adapted by our experiences and circumstances.
We feel like we are the same person we were years before, but we are not.

Grayson Perry, *Who Are You?* exhibition notes

Grayson Perry is a shapeshifter, gliding from one label to another. Through his work he constantly asks *Who am I?* and *Where am I?* Perry uses pottery, tapestry, painting and broadcasting as a means to unravel and examine both his own identity and that of the subjects who appear in his art. In his 2012 Channel 4 television series *In the Best Possible Taste*, Perry explores class, cultural differentiation and tribes. He is fascinated by what it means to both belong to and to escape from a tribe. His own autobiography blends with the narratives of his subjects, advocating tolerance and understanding. For someone with a humanities background, there can be no right answer just multiple possibilities. In his book *Playing to the Gallery*, as well as the BBC Radio *Reith Lectures* from which it is derived, he argues that we may be entering the age of pluralism. Extrapolating what he has learned from artistic exploration, he challenges: 'Wouldn't it be wonderful to believe that the pluralistic art world of the historical present was a harbinger for a political thing to come?'

This tolerance and pluralism is also evident in his 2014 Channel 4 series *Who Are You?* and the exhibition that accompanied it at the National Portrait Gallery in London. Questions of identity remain central, with Perry choosing as his theme individuals who are at a crossroads in their lives, whose sense of self has become fragmented, or who are building new identities for themselves. He describes his own role as part psychologist, part detective, as he converses with his subjects, photographs and sketches them, grows to understand them, then captures their essence in works of art. The blurring of boundaries, the redrawing of maps, the crossing of borders proliferate. Such motifs are evident in Perry's own cross-dressing identity, his adoption of the female alter ego Claire and his rake's progression from working-class roots to middle-class, art-world prestige. They are also the common denominator in his subjects' tales of religious self-discovery, gender change, celebrity and memory loss.

As an artist, Perry claims, he feels like a pilgrim on the road to meaning. In his biography *Portrait of the Artist as a Young Girl*, he speaks of escaping his own roots through art. Perry expounds on this further in 'The Rise and Fall of Default Man', a 2014 article published in *The New Statesman*. He points out that identity only seems to become an issue when it is challenged or under threat. He goes on to describe how the world is ruled by default men who make up the establishment. The default man is a defender of social norms, an upholder of rigid standards of conformity. Individuals like Perry, though, suffer from the imperative to create change and reject the status quo. They experiment, becoming part of what he refers to as a 'teasing rebellion'.

The *Who Are You?* exhibition illustrated this beautifully, proving to be a masterpiece of hyperlinking. Rather than housing the fourteen portraits – a mixture of ceramic urns, tapestries, etchings, sculptures and paintings – in one room, they were scattered through several rooms of the gallery's permanent display. They nestled alongside portraits of modernist writers and scholars, Victorian statesmen, military leaders and monarchs. They linked to the past while simultaneously subverting it. A giant tapestry, *Comfort Blanket*, questioned what it means to be British in a multi-ethnic, multi-faith, multi-class culture. In *Provincial Punk*, a career retrospective exhibition that followed in 2015 at the Turner Contemporary gallery in Margate, the boundary-crossing nature of the man and his work, his own pluralism, was made overt. The extraordinary *Map of Days*, featured at both exhibitions, is a self-portrait rendered as the street plan of a fortified town, hinting at the multidimensionality, contradictions and tensions of the person we know as Grayson Perry.

The very title of the *Provincial Punk* exhibition points to the meeting of the small-town art student with the do-it-yourself, learn-as you-go ethic that characterised punk and its New Romantic progeny. In *Punk: A Life Apart*, Stephen Colegrave and Chris Sullivan argue that for many involved in the musical and artistic scene that emerged in the 1970s, they recognised an opportunity to break free from social constraints, think for themselves and challenge the elitism and prejudices of older generations. As Joe Strummer of The Clash articulated it, 'I think people ought to know we're anti-fascist, we're anti-violence, we're anti-racist and we're pro-creative. We're against ignorance.' The punks sought autonomy and self-expression, a release from the remote control and dehumanisation of the factory and office. Through punk, Vivienne Westwood, another rural émigrée to the big city, transitioned from primary school teacher to fashion designer, discovering a vehicle and attitude for her activism.

Examining the cultural heritage of punk, Colegrave and Sullivan point to the influence of nineteenth-century French painter Gustave Courbet who believed that anyone could be a painter. They highlight too the influence of the Dada artistic movement of the 1920s, the Beat movement of the 1950s, Andy Warhol's Factory of the 1960s and musical trendsetters like David Bowie and The Velvet Underground. Through their collaboration and shared influence on punk, Westwood and Malcolm McLaren were drawing on antecedents as diverse as the Symbolist poet Rimbaud, the Situationists, the music and iconography of fifties rock, and their own experimentation with jewellery, clothing design and graphic art. In this context, a band could be an art installation, challenging people to see and hear in new ways. Inviting them to find their own voice too, to articulate their own desires and discontents, in however rudimentary a way, without fear of judgement. Artists, poets, musicians, fashion designers and theatrical performers exchanged ideas and roles, enabling a vibrant cultural exchange in which everyone was an apprentice, always learning. As James Watt suggests in *Business for Punks*, the movement, the approach to life that it fostered, was about acquiring the skills you needed to do things on your own terms.

The notion of bricolage and multimedia art forms took hold, expressed through live shows, cover art and posters, as well as torn clothing accessorised with pins, tape, images and the written word. The musical virtuosity of previous years was replaced by amateurism. Band members learned how to play even as they gained celebrity. Punk was inclusive and chaotic. With greater instrumental competence came exposure to and assimilation of a broader range of musical styles. Rock became hybridised with reggae, funk, rap and new wave pop; the sort of cosmopolitan, genre-defying music that characterises The Clash's *London Calling*. Pseudonyms were widely used as punks experimented with identity. Close connections and alliances were formed between punk and other countercultural, anti-establishment movements and performers. Everything was open to query, challenge and reinterpretation. David Byrne observes of the period, as he experimented with different looks and forms of musical expression, 'I was flailing about to see who I was'. It was a state of being that applied to many border-crossing, genre-defying figures including the punk poet Patti Smith, the punk fashion designer Westwood and the punk potter Perry.

As Byrne's personal insight suggests, the individual is shaped by experience, cultural context and personal metamorphosis; a constant becoming. Just as cultures are not static, neither are our identities. We construct the house we live in by figuring out what is worth doing and actively pursuing it. For Erika Ilves, it was work on a book that made her realise that humans are built to journey, not to arrive. *The Human Project*, co-authored with Anna Stillwell, examines the ultimate generalist question: What is the future of human civilisation? Determined to find answers, Erika spent years researching diverse fields that included evolutionary biology, history, anthropology, cosmology, psychology and science fiction. What started out as a conversation between two people evolved into a collaboration involving hundreds around the globe. *The Human Project* multimedia book and app were crowd-funded and licensed under the Creative Commons so that anyone can build on the ideas they contain.

The bridging of physical and mental borders, while not consciously pursued, was something that came naturally to Erika after years of constraint. The child of a Polish mother and Estonian father, she grew up in Tallinn under the shadow of the Cold War. Unable to leave until the collapse of the USSR, Erika started to spend two to three months abroad from the age of fifteen before leaving Estonia to study and work elsewhere when she turned nineteen. For a long time, she was conditioned by other people's expectations and frameworks. Dreams of becoming an astrophysicist, for example, were sidelined as she studied for a law degree, feeling the pressure to follow the path towards a more profitable career. Initial work as a lawyer soon gave way to management consultancy for established players like Deloitte and McKinsey. Based in Copenhagen, Johannesburg, Singapore and Sydney, Erika supported clients on strategy and innovation around the globe.

Erika is unbound by the mental shackles of specialisation. In conversations, she manoeuvres effortlessly in and out of topics like an experienced cab driver navigating the streets of the world's major cities. In matters of hard conceptual lifting, she resorts to finding the simplest words and expressions to convey her thoughts. She attributes broad reading habits to her ability to abstract details from a general pattern and transmit ideas in a relatable way. With a thousand books stored on her Kindle, she draws from a big tank of metaphors outside of people's normal level of abstraction. When working as a management consultant, there was a high demand for this skill from clients who relied on her observant nature to help them understand why they existed, what they should do and where they should go next.

After six years with McKinsey, Erika moved on first to Oslo, then Dubai, then London. New experiences altered her sense of belonging, her understanding of who she was and what she was becoming, as she also tried on different professional roles as a business executive, entrepreneur and consultant. Crossing between futurism, innovation, leadership and strategy gave her meaningful direction and intellectual stimulation. Erika increasingly challenged her clients to incorporate a wider perspective into their solutions, to reconceive their role in the world, leaving behind a lasting contribution to society, an enduring legacy. From her professional practice, she gained clarity about her personal *why*, which eventually led her to *The Human Project*.

A visionary tour de force, *The Human Project* frames sixteen entangled challenges and evolutionary opportunities that could significantly impact our survival and ascent as a species. The underpinning purpose of the project is to create awareness about the most important issues facing humanity and establish an actionable framework, a grounded vision for 2050. *Who are we humans? Who should we become? Where should we head to next?* In the pursuit of answers to these questions, it became clear to Erika that most challenges and opportunities were looked at in isolation by experts, who prioritised their own areas of interest to the detriment of others. Diverse topics relating to climate change, food and water shortages, poverty, war, overpopulation, terrorism and economic crises were competing for attention. At the same time, there was little overlap or connection between initiatives focused on space-faring civilisation, transhumanism, a zero-carbon world, artificial intelligence and universal human rights. Few were interested in looking beyond their own field of specialism, in attaining a holistic overview and seeing the future of humanity in context.

For Erika, the five years it took to develop and realise the book project was a time of transformation, a journey into the unknown, the impossible, the unimaginable. It took the notion of stretch goals on to another level. Most of what is outlined in *The Human Project* will take multiple decades, in some cases several lifetimes, to achieve. Erika has chosen to focus her own efforts on space settlement, the challenge she believes will have the biggest impact when resolved. It is a massive undertaking to recreate a biosphere on Mars or the Moon or elsewhere; one that will require that we succeed in establishing a closed loop system where survival is not dependent on support from Earth. If we can figure it out, it will not only allow us to extract minerals and energy but has the potential to lead us to viable solutions for cleaning up our own biosphere. What started out as small steps on Erika's personal journey ultimately could amount to one giant leap for humankind extending beyond her own life expectancy.

Through her writing and research, Erika has become integrated into a broad network of entrepreneurs working on establishing an interplanetary society. She has gone on to co-found two companies. The Shackleton Energy Company is working on three challenges in space: energy, water and internet access. It aims to establish a global consortium of public and private partners to invest $18 billion in resolving them. Transplanetary is developing an Artificial Intelligence-powered platform that will provide real-time insight for investors, analysts and enthusiasts in the emergent commercial space community. Mobilising different industries and governments to make an impact on any of the sixteen challenges and opportunities that are explored in *The Human Project* is an extremely complex task. Space is still an unfathomable concept for most people. To address it, Erika relies on symbiotic relationships, drawing on the deep expertise of the specialists even as her own neo-generalism serves to expand their understanding of how what they do and aspire to fits into a broader vision of the future.

As Erika's international wanderings taught her, places influence who we are and how others perceive us. Escaping the boundaries set by conditions and place of birth is a prominent driver for many neo-generalists. The quest for a place to be ourselves is central in Taiye Selasi's work as an author, photographer, documentary maker and playwright. The elder of twin girls, she was born in London and moved to Brookline, Massachusetts, when she was eight. Her mother is a paediatrician with Nigerian heritage and her father is a surgeon and poet with Ghanaian heritage. Selasi was educated in American Studies at Yale University then studied International Relations at Oxford University. She is a citizen of many worlds with more than one home and an identity based on a mosaic of local experiences.

In her TED Talk, *Don't ask where I'm from, ask where I'm a local*, Selasi illustrates how important experiences are in shaping our identity. She believes we can never go back to a place and find it where we left it. We can only see the world through the eyes we have in the moment, influenced by where we have been and by the people we have been with – and, most importantly, by the person we have become. Time moves on. Something, somewhere, will always have changed. Most of all ourselves. We derive a sense of *being local* from the places where we carry out our rituals and relationships. But also from restrictions, from where we are able to live with the passport that we hold, from the constrained conditions under which we can thrive and grow. Selasi herself derives meaning from being multi-local in four locations spread across three continents. Characters and places reflected in her writing can be found in a supermarket in Trastevere in Rome, a brief encounter in the streets of Berlin, suburban life in New Jersey or her mother's tranquil garden in Accra.

Like Selasi, Solonia Teodros and Grace Clapham have had to construct, deconstruct and reconstruct their identities many times over. 'Home is not where you were born; home is where all your attempts to escape cease', states the Egyptian writer and novelist Naguib Mahfouz. For Solonia and Grace, that place is the Change School which they co-founded, and the life it has enabled as 'changepreneurs'. Their common history as childhood friends and their diverse life experiences have merged into a higher purpose. As business partners, the essence of their achievements is relational. It is founded upon and respects both their similarities and differences. While they balance one another on the extroversion–introversion spectrum, they are typically neo-generalist in their responsiveness to the contextual need for generalism and specialism.

As third-culture kids, a term coined in the 1960s by sociologist Ruth Hill Useem, both Solonia and Grace have spent most of their formative years outside of their parent's culture. Solonia, for example, was born to Taiwanese and Ethiopian parents but holds US citizenship. She grew up in Boston and relocated to Taipei at the age of nine. In Taiwan, she often found herself on the receiving end of glares and curious questions about her origin. Mastery of three languages did not prevent her from getting lost in translation at the borderline between Eastern and Western values. On a daily basis, she had to adapt to different rules at home and in school. By attending international schools in Taiwan and Singapore, Solonia developed a high sensitivity towards the subtle cultural nuances carried in a name or reflected in a skin colour. So accustomed did she become to the rich diversity of her closest friends, that it was not until she went to university in the USA that she gained a new perspective on the multicultural lifestyle she had enjoyed growing up. What had been normal was suddenly rendered exotic.

As a graduate with a degree in International Relations from Boston University, Solonia struggled to find a job in her area of specialism. While she had always been told her experiences and language skills would set her up for life, recruiters did not acknowledge her wide cross-cultural upbringing. Instead, she dabbled in multiple fields as a research assistant, photo studio manager and strategy consultant in Boston and New York before returning to Asia. A short stint at a public relations agency in Singapore exposed her to a highly competitive work place. For someone who appreciated collaboration and preferred to wear flip flops rather than Jimmy Choos it was a demoralising experience. Unable to invest her soul in spinning stories and making brands look good, Solonia decided to start her own agency with an emphasis on guiding social entrepreneurs and curating communal events in Singapore.

Grace's background and upbringing is similarly diverse. She was born in Jakarta to an Indonesian-Dutch mother and an Australian father. She lived in Jakarta until she was five and moved to Singapore, staying there till the age of eleven. In Quito, Ecuador, Grace attended a Spanish-speaking school for a year and stayed in the Galapagos Islands, living on a boat, before her family made its way back to Singapore. She finished high school in Australia and graduated from the University of Melbourne with a degree in Media and Communications, spending a gap year working in London and Paris. Grace returned to Singapore in 2009 to set up her first business, Agent Grace. For two years, she operated as an independent brand management and marketing adviser to fashion, travel and lifestyle enterprises seeking to establish themselves in the Singapore region.

When Grace's father passed away in 2013, she realised it was time to reconfigure and redesign her life, opting to focus her future work on the intersections between communities, collaboration, impact and change. Her ambition was to connect individuals and cultures and create opportunities for local talents to reach their potential on a global level. Grace is never just doing one thing. She builds communities and ecosystems for women and creative entrepreneurs. She mentors start-ups and runs the Change School. Locality is also a theme in Grace's identity. Her life is triangulated by three places. Singapore is a vibrant cultural melting pot, offering new business opportunities and a space to socialise, connect the dots and learn with others. Jakarta is both birthplace and disorientation, a space to explore and observe the quirkiness of life. Peace, tranquillity and regeneration is what she takes away from Bali. In those three locations, her personal and professional preferences intersect and offer adjacent possibilities as she takes ideas from one area and moves them into a new context.

In our modern world, the meaning we derive from our geographical origin and professional career is changing. Technological development, over the last twenty-five years in particular, has created an age of extraordinary freedom and choice. With the Internet, our radius of cultural influences has expanded. In the past, locality was the area where we grew up, now it also encompasses the world that is digitally connected to us. The notion of living a heathy life in a digital world and making conscious choices about the things we pay attention to, is a recurring theme for Solonia and Grace. In 2015, the Change School inaugurated the first Third Culture Kid Summit in Rajasthan, India. The event kick-started a year-long exploration of what it means to be a third-culture kid and brought together a wide range of leading thinkers, entrepreneurs, cultural explorers and academics. The event connected Solonia and Grace with Eddie Harran.

Another third-culture kid, Eddie grew up in Australia, the USA and New Zealand with an Irish father and a Japanese mother. He is among a growing number of people who consider themselves nomads. After graduating from the University of Queensland, Eddie backpacked for a year in southern Asia and later spent six years experimenting with different jobs as a speaker, futurist, catalyst and network weaver. Like someone bound to Campbell's monomyth, he regularly leaves one world in order to enter another, never ending, always becoming. The ambiguity and uncertainty that comes from shifting between locations, work and relationships has taught him to be adaptable and flexible. Present-day nomads are extensions of Peter Drucker's *knowledge workers* concept; individuals that leverage technology in order to work remotely and live an independent and itinerant lifestyle. Lower costs of living and higher quality of life drive this movement. Nomads occupy a self-constructed space outside of the familiar hierarchies of traditional organisations where work and life are integrated. They typically operate in creative jobs as social media experts, bloggers, writers, filmmakers, coders, web developers or designers.

Eddie's home is where the crowd is. As an experienced liminal surfer he has developed a preference for living in a state of perpetual beta, receptive to the unknown and aware that truth is contextually relative. Questions of belonging, being and becoming are ever-present for him as he flows in and out of networks like 'an ecosystems diplomat'. He curates knowledge through play while advancing his understanding of the world and finding his place in it. In a digital environment, the concept of identity is an issue of much greater complexity than it was in the pre-Internet era. Our identity in the digital space can exist in many forms and for many different purposes. On the back of his experiences with the WisdomHackers.com community, Eddie created a philosophical, online alter ego called Dr Time. He refers to this persona as a Timescape Sensemaker; an identity used to explore how our individual perspectives of time affect our work, health and well-being. Shifting between roles as co-creator of and participant in communities, Eddie leverages relationships to share experiences, string together ideas and learn through conversations with others.

Generous in sharing insights from his research and personal experiences, Eddie is one of life's givers. A network navigator and facilitator who keeps knowledge and ideas moving. In his book *Give and Take*, Wharton professor Adam Grant describes three human orientations in life. *Takers* like to receive more than they give. They tend to be self-focused and preoccupied with what others can offer them, demanding help but rarely offering it themselves. *Matchers* operate from a position of quid pro quo, expecting something in return if they help. *Givers* strive to be generous with their time, energy, knowledge, skills, ideas and connections. They contribute to others without expecting anything in return. According to Grant, the most successful people are givers who care about others and, at the same time, stick to their own interests.

Tamar Many has made a career out of such generosity, forming institutional partnerships in the academic field. Throughout her life, Tamar has invariably found herself traversing the boundaries between different worlds, whether those are geographic locations or disciplines. Born into a medical family in Israel, she grew up in the USA where her father, a leading gastroenterologist, led a renowned institute that developed a simple solution for the complex problem of malnutrition in Third World countries. As a child, Tamar was exposed to an international environment, travelling often as her father was required to share his learning and experience with physicians all over the world. She quickly acquired her parents' deep interest in the arts too. At the age of eighteen, she returned to Israel to study at Bezalel Academy of Art and Design in Jerusalem from where she graduated with a degree in Graphic Design.

Tamar's interest in design and visual communication led her to co-found Textured Paper, a company that specialises in artistic greetings cards. These are sold at galleries like the Museum of Modern Art in New York. Alongside her entrepreneurial endeavour, Tamar started teaching visual communication and design, first at Bezalel, then at Shenkar College of Engineering and Design in Tel Aviv. Shenkar's focus is on research, innovation and originality. The college is a creative hub that combines conceptual and technical skills with an interdisciplinary approach to engineering, textile printing and fashion design. It makes use of techniques both from artisanal crafts and high-end technologies. As a teacher, Tamar urges her students to cross boundaries in their thinking. She mixes classes to create a learning environment where diverse ideas are welcomed, understood, included and valued. Her students study nature to enhance their design perspectives. They expand the possibilities of collaboration by engaging in interdisciplinary projects where each sub-speciality informs the result. They create novel projects by transforming ideas from the past.

Tamar has applied the same curiosity and compassion for people in a different field since taking over as director of International Studies and Relations at Shenkar in 2014. Within a short period of time, the school has managed to form partnerships with some of the world's most renowned academic institutions. Much like her father who started out as a specialist and later on became a wise synthesiser of knowledge, a practitioner and a scholar, Tamar's identity is also one with many layers. Her greatest interest is in getting people to work together, creating beautiful designs from fragmented pieces.

The shifts in working and educational practices that we are witnessing today suggest a future founded upon such fragmentation, characterised by what David Weinberger has termed *small pieces loosely joined*. In such a scenario, knowledge resides in the network rather than with any one individual. Loose collectives, temporary confederacies, are formed to deliver projects and then disbanded. The organisational core shrinks, serving as a platform, a hub, within larger networks of business partners, many of whom operate in different spaces and at different times. In some cases, organisations may become wholly atomised, broken up into small pieces that re-cohere for short-term work. Freelancers, consultancies and other suppliers orbit around the organisational core.

A new sort of tension manifests itself. On the one hand, there is the sense of tribal belonging, of identity derived from association with a corporate entity and the communal interaction related to it. On the other, there is a need for personal agency, for individual autonomy and growth, unrestrained by the organisational trappings of policy, process and regulation. The Self Agency, founded by Anne McCrossan and her friend Simon Gough, addresses this shift in our working lives. Its people-first approach values the individual before the impersonality of the corporate institution. It seeks to build an unfettered community that fosters creativity and the development of digital literacy. It recognises human diversity, individuality and quirkiness, as well as our need for connection and interaction with others. In doing so, it addresses fundamental questions. How do we achieve a sense of belonging, while simultaneously giving expression to our own identity? How do we accept uniqueness rather than imposing uniformity? How do we maintain mental agility?

Conformity and habitual thinking are widespread in our society because they are convenient. Energy is preserved in the denial of movement and by refusing to see the unexpected cracks and imperfections that are presented to us in our daily lives. Left unattended, habits trap us, like Bill Murray's character in *Groundhog Day*, in a repetitive mode enacting the same routines day in and day out. In *Herd*, Mark Earls makes the point that it is human nature to imitate group behaviours in order to blend in and gain acceptance. We form herds for many self-interested reasons. Groups afford protection. In greater numbers, we are usually safer and stronger. It is a natural tendency evident among many other species too. Starlings form murmurations to protect themselves from predators and lions employ a cooperative hunting tactic, in which some drive the prey towards others in the pride waiting to ambush them. By sticking together, we harness power, knowledge and resources to achieve collective benefits and address the big issues we encounter. Shared interests, vision and purpose provide a sense of belonging and secure protection by the group.

Robert Putman, in his book *Bowling Alone*, speaks of two ways of thinking about social capital, which he describes in terms of *bridging* and *bonding*. Bridging is the process of making friends with like-spirited people where we benefit from differences in worldviews and skills, and connect through similar values, ethics and visions. Bonding, by contrast, occurs when we form relationships with people who agree with us and affirm our convictions. Bonding is linked to living in neighbourhoods with people of the same social status and having the same nationality, race and religion. But it also relates to consuming information that feeds our preconceptions and caters to our pre-existing values. If we are to live a fulfilling life, both bridging and bonding are required. It is bridging, though, that earns the highest rewards, that pushes society forward.

In our personal lives we switch in and out of roles as fathers, daughters, friends, colleagues and lovers. We learn that we can be different things to different people in a variety of different contexts. But in our professional lives this is rarely recognised, making it difficult to translate a diversified career into a coherent narrative or service that others can relate to. Most neo-generalists have encountered situations in which their expertise falls outside neat corporate categorisation. Others struggle to recognise their unique perspectives and how their multifaceted talents can benefit their organisations. Labels only speak to who we are at a given time and place. They are constrained by context, never capturing the full essence of individual complexity and potential. 'Are you a space person now?', people asked Erika Ilves after she pivoted in her career. 'She is not a true Ghanaian', people said of Taiye Selasi when she published her first book *Ghana Must Go*. These examples show that singular definitions are often of greater importance to the definers than to the defined. When asked who they are today, both Erika and Taiye simply reply: *I am human*.

Identity and identification share an etymology, derived from *idem*, Latin for *the same*. It refers to the constant balancing of the need to be part of something greater than ourselves and the desire to be independent, autonomous creators of our own destiny. Like a two-way street, traffic moves in either direction, going out from ourselves and coming back towards us from others. As Walt Whitman phrases it in 'Song of Myself', *For every atom belonging to me as good belongs to you*. Identity is a balance of competing interests and impulses for the neo-generalist. Conformity can limit the worlds between which they can travel. Yet, separation and questioning of the status quo can carry the risk of being ejected from the group that provides safety and a sense of belonging. Even living at the edge, there is a desire to be one of the small pieces connected to the ever-shifting whole.

Their inner world not only influences, but is paramount to how the neo-generalist sees the outer world, how their ethics are shaped, and how they perceive and act upon the opportunities that emerge in life. Personal purpose is intricately connected with broader cultural movements and future aspirations. In the pursuit of individual goals, they service collective possibilities, contributing through word and deed as writers, speakers, teachers, entrepreneurs and leaders. Theirs is a thorough exploration of the questions *Who am I?* and *Where am I?* A balancing act between introspection and outrospection. Their encounters with and internalisation of the unexpected and the unknown has enabled them to adapt to constraints, to shapeshift, to redraw maps for both themselves and those who choose to follow them.

7.
SHORING
FRAGMENTS

*These fragments I have shored
against my ruins*

T. S. Eliot, *The Waste Land*

The first two decades of the twentieth century were subject to seismic shifts. Wherever you looked change was afoot. The established world order began to falter, political ideologies to evolve, rulers to be overthrown, new superpowers to emerge. The suffrage movement made inroads into the electoral system. Scientific discovery opened to question what was known about space, time and the mind. Archaeological and anthropological discovery expanded understanding of our ancestors. Technological innovation in communication and transportation shrank the world. Industrialisation began to take hold on a grand scale, evident in car manufacture, the cinema and warfare. Modernist experimentation was rife in the arts affecting painting, theatre, photography, dance, film and music. Little was coherent. Everything was in a state of turmoil. The reverberations of the Great War carried on into the new decade: the Ottoman Empire was dismantled, fascism took root, economies fluctuated then crashed dramatically. Telephones and radio expanded the information networks, disseminating new forms of popular culture like jazz.

As Kevin Jackson relates in *Constellation of Genius*, 1922 proved to be a seminal year in literary modernism, as it caught up with the stylistic and thematic experimentation evident elsewhere in the arts. The year was bookended by two major publications that would echo through the remainder of the century and beyond, heavily influencing the modernist and postmodern authors that followed. First was the publication of James Joyce's epic novel *Ulysses*, which was followed by T. S. Eliot's poem *The Waste Land*. Formally innovative, these works synthesised ideas from new science with ancient mythology, making use of cultural and sociopolitical allusion to elide temporal, spatial and personal boundaries, to blend Christian, Ancient Greek and Eastern philosophies. Through a diversity and intermingling of sources, they examined and critiqued modern life, jumping from the personal to the collective, from the high-brow to the mundane, mixing different voices, different languages, like a radio skipping through numerous international frequencies.

In collating allusive fragments within their own pages, these works also engendered a legacy that would manifest itself across a range of nationalities and forms of cultural expression. The shadow of *Ulysses*, for example, looms over the literary output of the Latin American magical realists. The influence of *The Waste Land* is evident in the cinematic *Chinatown* and the novelistic *The Crying of Lot 49*. Its influence on the visual arts is the subject of a project managed by curators at the Turner Contemporary gallery in Margate, one of the sites of Eliot's composition of the poem, who plan to dedicate an exhibition to the topic in 2018. What literary works like *The Waste Land* underscore is that we are all an assembly of what we have read, the people we have met, the places we have visited, the conversations we have had, the work we have done, the shared experiences and recollected histories of the communities in which we live. Our identities are constantly shifting, evolving, reassembling these disparate pieces. We shore our own fragments against our personal ruins, our myriad selves.

The neo-generalist is always looking for inspiration elsewhere. It might be from other disciplines, through the combinatory play of mixing art with science, listening to music, reading or playing sport. It might, as leadership development and learning analyst Adina Forsström frames it, relate to learning about life through other people. Working alongside them, observing them, interacting with them, imitating them, adapting what they do for our own purposes. What is learned elsewhere is absorbed and internalised. In *How Music Works*, David Byrne discusses how he and his colleagues would look to other mediums, to fine art, poetry and circus shows, for ideas that could inform their own compositions and performance. When you live in many worlds, sometimes there is no need to look any further than your own multidimensional experiences. In his genre-bending fiction, for example, James Sallis is able to draw on personal knowledge derived as respiratory therapist, musicologist, translator and poet to enrich his narratives. The salvage of his own yesterdays, to paraphrase his novel *Death Will Have Your Eyes*, underpins the fictional worlds he creates.

Sallis's diverse experiences are emblematic of the slash-career that Marci Alboher explores in her book *One Person/Multiple Careers*. Since at least the late 1960s, Sallis has self-identified as a creative writer. This is at the core of both his identity and his career, evidenced by his numerous novels, short story volumes and poetry collections. However, either through economic necessity, a desire to give back to the community or the pursuit of a personal passion, Sallis has added further strings to his bow. Sometimes these fall loosely under the man-of-letters banner, including his work as essayist, columnist and biographer. Lecturing in colleges, working in hospitals and performing as a musician, however, are all quite distinct slash-careers that at one time or another have been added to his portfolio.

Alboher's analysis similarly highlights people who have arrived at intriguing career combinations in their pursuit of an economically-viable and meaningful life. Among her subjects, for example, are Mary Mazzio whose portfolio includes a past as an Olympic rower and a present as both lawyer and filmmaker; Robert Childs who is a psychotherapist and violin maker; and Karen Rispoli who is a career coach, bus driver and private investigator. Alboher's evolving argument complements social philosopher Charles Handy's attempts to distinguish between paid endeavour, charitable work, study and household chores, as well as poet David Whyte's examination of the three marriages with a partner, self and career. All introduce different types of slashes.

The notion of a kaleidoscopic career, of many fragments cohering into clearly focused images, is explored further by Ian Sanders and David Sloly in *Mash-up*. They make a case for the harmonious blending of different career opportunities. The metaphors they use resonate strongly with many of our own interviewees. Researcher and digital explorer Rotana Ty, for example, in reflecting on his own experiences living on the specialist–generalist continuum and adapting to contextual shifts, makes reference to the disc-jockey concept favoured by Sanders and Sloly. A DJ, particularly in the era that followed the emergence of hip hop in the late 1970s, constantly borrows from, samples and remixes existing music to create something new. They do in music what the modernist authors of the 1920s were doing in literature; stealing like artists, as Austin Kleon phrases it.

Lars Wetterberg is drawn to an alternative analogy. Lars has combined an academic background in psychology with an extensive career in the field of corporate learning and development. He speaks of the many pieces of a jigsaw puzzle that make up the whole person. The diverse interests and practices reflect different aspects of the continuum, which itself offers a 360-degree perspective of the individual moving through spacetime. Each element can be shuffled and resampled in fresh and interesting ways. New puzzles are always in the making. In another variation, business adviser, analyst and occasional jazz pianist Jane McConnell favours the metaphor of the drinks mixologist, who like a DJ crafts something unique from creative integration.

The neo-generalist is ever curious, painting pictures, telling stories, mixing, sampling, experimenting, trying to redraw the edges of the map. They absorb influences from diverse sources and gain wide experience from practice in multiple fields. Through their digital and analogue wanderings, they also learn to spot gaps, the cracks through which the trickster passes, the opportunities for innovation. Nevertheless, such innovation is largely determined by and dependent upon what already exists. It is subject to creative constraint, loose frameworks. Creativity manifests itself in the ways people build on, develop and reshape that which has come before. This is very much the thesis of Christian Stadil and Lene Tanggaard in *In the Shower with Picasso*. They illustrate how creative people operate on the edge of, rather than outside, the box. They may well serve as bridges to new ideas and outside influence, their efforts may well result in the map being redrawn, but essentially they continue to operate within the recognisable bounds of their discipline. It is a notion supported by filmmaker Michael Powell.

During the 1940s, Powell was one half of a formidable partnership with Emeric Pressburger. Through their production company, The Archers, they created some of the classics of British cinema, including *The Life and Death of Colonel Blimp, A Canterbury Tale, A Matter of Life and Death* and *The Red Shoes*. They were mavericks who sought to defy industry conventions, using the constraints imposed by a studio system, limited budgets, censorship and wartime propaganda as a catalyst to creativity. Sharing credits for writing, direction and production, Powell and Pressburger were highly literate filmmakers who tried to blend film, art, music, dance, theatre, poetry and fiction into a synaesthetic cinematic experience. They were ahead of their time, pushing the envelope of what was possible in the medium. Their appeal was broad and their willingness to think and operate differently, to go against convention, was recognised and celebrated by subsequent generations of filmmakers. Yet, for all their experimentation with film form and content, what The Archers did was build in a progressive way on the foundations of more conformist antecedents in the industry. They innovated at the edges, still operating within the system, seeking to change it from the inside out. Tellingly, Powell observed in his autobiography that if 'originality and truth are your aim, cultivate your own back garden'.

This is a theme picked up by the chef René Redzepi, who is one of the owners of the Copenhagen restaurant Noma. Alboher argues that celebrity chefs are prime examples of individuals who pursue multifaceted careers, using cuisine as the main hub for their endeavours. As these chefs experience success, they diversify and add further spokes. They open more restaurants, offer masterclasses, write books, launch product lines associated with their brand, host television shows dedicated to the art and science of cooking. Redzepi has certainly strayed into some of this territory, co-authoring books, helping others to develop their culinary craft, but the vision he shares with colleagues at Noma is shaped by a higher purpose. This has centred on the reinvigoration of Nordic Cuisine and a sustainable approach to fine dining that is largely dependent on foraging and locally sourced ingredients. During its first twelve years, Noma enjoyed phenomenal success. It earned two Michelin stars and was garlanded on four occasions by *Restaurant* magazine as the best eating establishment in the world.

Despite the plaudits, Redzepi and his team have continued to explore how to improve their sustainability mission. They refuse to stand still, constantly looking for cracks, for opportunities to be more creative. To this end, Redzepi issued a video announcement in 2015 titled *A Very Short Film About the Past, Present and Future of Noma*. In it he outlines the restaurant's overarching philosophy, its Nordic identity spanning the North Atlantic region from Scandinavia to Greenland, its fusion of traditional Nordic dishes with international ingredients like potatoes and chocolate, its research efforts in the fields of food science and innovation, and its connection to the region's land and sea. Setting out a direction of travel for Noma's future, Redzepi describes how the restaurant will close its current establishment in a waterfront warehouse in the Christianshavn neighbourhood at the end of 2016 and move to a nearby site in Christiania where they can accommodate their new Noma restaurant and enhanced research facilities, as well as grow their own produce too.

Noma's menu will become more closely aligned with seasonal shifts: vegetarian dishes will be served in late Spring and early Summer, game dishes in the Autumn, fish and seafood during the Winter months. Both kitchen staff and diners will adapt to the dramatic transformations in the Nordic seasons. Not only will Noma aspire to the embodiment of regional identity, but it will attempt to capture the flavour of the landscape at different points in time, echoing the rhythms of nature, sensitive to the interacting systems that surround its man-made operation. The idea is that Noma and its people become fragments in a sustainable environmental system, respectful and nurturing of the local ecology; an inversion of the industrialised systems of the past. It is a vision of the future that is neo-generalist in its pursuit of new questions, its synthesis of different information and practices, its leap between culinary specialisms on a seasonal basis, its harnessing of diverse skill sets and produce, and its empathic approach towards both people and the natural world.

Systems thinking underpins Noma's proposed reinvention. It is also at the core of Hans-Jürgen Sturm's approach to learning and work. Hans-Jürgen has fulfilled a number of different information management and digital transformation roles at Amadeus since the turn of the century. Amadeus is a large travel technology organisation that manages a global distribution system enabling many different aspects of the travel experience, covering searches, reservations and check-in procedures. The company partners with an array of other organisations in the travel sector, including travel agencies, corporate travel services, hotels, airlines and railway operators. The environment in which the company functions is one of complex interacting systems all harnessed in service of the customer.

Hans-Jürgen has drawn on his academic background, which includes an initial degree in Geography and a PhD in Tropical Ecology, to shape his understanding of corporate ecosystems and how things connect. He uses this insight to navigate and guide others through the electronic marketplace and social business landscape in which he now operates. He also speaks of the formative impact of his voluntary and research experiences working as a young man in Western Africa. As a European in another continent, he describes the 'schizophrenic effect' of bridging two different cultures, indicating a heightened sensitivity to the varied approaches to time and human relationships.

The neo-generalist wanderer often has to adapt to contextual shifts and reinvent themselves when circumstances call for it. Lucas Amungwa, for example, never imagined that he would one day return home to farm in Cameroon when he graduated with a master's degree in Applied Microbiology and Biotechnology from the University of Wolverhampton. Lucas went on to work for a couple of years at a pharmaceutical company in the UK as a scientific officer specialising in animal vaccines, before then enrolling on a PhD programme in microbiology at the University of Essex. His trajectory towards a career associated with deep specialism was disrupted, however, by external factors over which he had little control. Lucas was accustomed to supporting himself as a student, making ends meet through ad hoc employment. In the wake of the financial crash, though, the UK government suspended grants for international students and tightened the immigration policies, effectively prohibiting him from working in England as a foreign student. Reluctantly, he found he had to withdraw from further postgraduate studies.

Back in Cameroon, Lucas found that he had a significant role to play in an evolving narrative. His father, Julius Martin Amungwa, had trained as an agronomist, maintaining an interest in acquiring and cultivating land near his native village Bambili even as he had pursued a successful and high-ranking career in the Cameroonian military. Julius Martin had unexpectedly passed away following a brief illness not long after Lucas's graduation from Wolverhampton. The fallout from his demise and the claims being placed on his landholdings were escalating as Lucas returned to Cameroon from Essex. Although the fourth born of five children, Lucas found himself assuming a leadership role, navigating a complex and tension-laden intersection between modernity and tradition. Julius Martin's purchases, often secured with verbal agreements rather than formal documentation, had been intended as a legacy for his children. His investments had increased in value as Bambili had transformed from rural village into a vibrant university town. The allure of land was something that others with a vested interest in the extended family could not ignore.

As Lucas tackled issues concerning land rights, he simultaneously reinvented himself as an agricultural entrepreneur focused in particular on plantain and poultry farming. With little prior experience in the field, but with the foundation of his academic research and the curiosity of a neo-generalist, Lucas mainly relied on experiential and social learning. He quickly realised that skills and experience acquired elsewhere were transferable and had utility in new contexts. Lucas bridged between and cross-pollinated two distinct worlds. He read scientific papers about farming in Brazil and Nigeria, as well as carrying out field trips to test the quality of local products. He engaged in detailed conversations with farmers in the community that helped him understand rainfall patterns, soil conditions, fluctuations in temperature, supply chains and local workers. Lucas blended knowledge of animal husbandry with biological insights about decomposition and microorganisms. A willingness to experiment, to explore uncharted territory, resulted in the discovery of new ways to crossbreed chickens and turn toxic waste into organic manure that could be used in plantain cultivation.

Lucas's new identity was shaped by this fusion of his academic background and his evolving practice in the regional agriculture, as well as by his mediation role within the extended family. In the latter capacity, he found himself dealing with issues of kinship and the concept of Ubuntu; of the connection of humanity through a universal bond of sharing. Ubuntu is concerned with deeply rooted fellowship and interconnectedness. People are expected to live their lives in ways that ensure that others may live well too: *I am, because we are*. It was, for example, a philosophy that underpinned the administration of the Truth and Reconciliation Commission chaired by Desmond Tutu in post-Apartheid South Africa. Ubuntu underscores the mutual dependence between humans to survive and thrive. Through taking care of others and your surroundings, you take care of yourself. However, Ubuntu blurs the traditional boundaries of ownership known elsewhere in the world. It was the exploitation of these boundaries by his uncles that Lucas had to address, taking into account both patriarchal tradition and modern law.

At the core of the dispute between Lucas's widowed mother and his uncles was the expectation, in keeping with local tradition, that what Julius Martin had owned effectively belonged to Lucas's grandfather. When Lucas's father died, therefore, his uncles made a claim on his land because of the grandparental birth right. The lack of legal documentation only complicated matters. Lucas sought to reconcile the dilemmas caused by greed and envy. As his father's successor, he faced the challenge of balancing his own self-interest with the interests of many others, simultaneously working as disruptor and diplomat. The time Lucas spent studying and living abroad had given him a fresh perspective that set him apart from others in the village. As an outsider, he regularly met with elders in the community to seek their advice. He became a student of relationships, of learning to reframe from different points of view, achieving balance between diametrically opposed positions. Ultimately, the land dispute was resolved through dialogue and firm action. In the process, Lucas gained self-awareness and a strong sense of values, learning to respect tradition even as he gently subverted it with modern ideas, ensuring that the individual could not be oppressed by the collective.

F. Scott Fitzgerald once observed, 'the test of a first-rate intelligence is the ability to hold two opposed ideas in the mind at the same time, and still retain the ability to function'. Neo-generalists like Lucas are whole-brain thinkers with a both/and rather than an either/or perspective. Anand Mahindra, honoured as one of the world's fifty greatest leaders by *Fortune* magazine, also embodies this kind of complementarity thinking. Anand spent his formative years abroad pursuing a film studies major at Harvard College, and later attaining an MBA from Harvard Business School. He then returned to India to join the Mahindra family business, which had been founded by his grandfather in 1945. Anand credits his liberal arts education for his whole-brain approach to management. He believes that a balance between intuition and logic enables him to perceive larger patterns and adopt a fresh approach to opportunities. Outside the office he continues to take a keen interest in music and filmmaking, and has founded film and blues festivals in Mumbai.

Liberal arts have become essential to shaping leaders of the future in the Mahindra Group, with a strong emphasis on mental flexibility and whole-brain thinking incorporated into the group's leadership development activities. Good decision-making is reliant on our ability to look beyond our company's industry for insight and to interpret what we find, while retaining the ability to question and challenge, avoiding the trap of confirmation bias or the myopia of deep specialism. Anand himself comes across as interesting because he is genuinely interested. It is noticeable in the way that he asks questions that curiosity is what motivates him. In conversation, he listens observantly, ready to pick up and play with thought-provoking ideas. One way Anand stays current with emerging trends is through a diligent use of social media. With nearly three million followers on Twitter, he leverages the platform to share ideas, listen for weak signals and scan the horizon for usable knowledge. It extends his reach beyond organisational boundaries and enables him to synthesise information from a wide range of sources.

Anand is a firm believer in enabling human potential. As with Ubuntu, the achievements of the individual benefits all; the success of the corporation services the broader community. At a personal level, Anand focuses on the contribution he makes, rather than the direction he gives to others. What began as a steel trading company, under his tenure as chairman and managing director has grown into a federation of companies with over 200,000 employees and a presence in more than one hundred countries. The Mahindra Group operates across a range of sectors including the automotive, farm equipment, financial services, IT, aerospace, real estate, energy and defence industries. Each company under the Mahindra umbrella is a node in a larger network. They are independent entities with their own boards and governance, blending Eastern and Western management philosophies, and combining the strengths of both specialism and generalism. When the Mahindra Group restructured into a federation of companies in 1994, it was in response to the liberalisation of the Indian market. Part of the inspiration came from the way private equity firms manage a broad portfolio. Through diversification the organisation rendered itself more responsive and less vulnerable to shifts in the market. Corporate fragments brought together in common purpose and united by shared values. Mutuality enabled at a macro level.

Kare Anderson is an award-winning journalist based in San Francisco. She provides guidance on building a mutuality mindset and serving others as opportunity makers. Kare is attuned to how different pieces connect, observing how people cultivate friendships with those who have complementary skills and temperaments, even where their worldviews diverge. Clarity about and appreciation of respective talents can result in a fertile inter-section between people and ideas. It places the individual in a collective context, bound through open-mindedness and a gener-osity of spirit. There is a striking resonance with Ubuntu in Kare's ideas: without *we* there can be no *me*; what Baudelaire refers to as 'an ego athirst for the non-ego' in *The Painter of Modern Life*. By opening themselves up to a diversity of influences and connec-tions, the individual becomes part of a rich network, with knowl-edge and influence ebbing and flowing as the needs of different constituent elements are serviced. It is with the perspective of the many that opportunities can be discerned and acted upon. There is always some part of the network that will derive benefit as a consequence. The neo-generalist has a role as catalyst, connector and messenger in such an environment, traversing bridges and nodes, enabling knowledge and ideas to flow, bringing people together and moving them to action.

This is a role that Peter Vander Auwera fulfils, wandering between different worlds, advocating change agency and innovation, bringing a humanities-oriented perspective to a domain gov-erned by economics and technology. Peter currently works in the FinTech industry, but is also an artist who thinks of himself as an impresario, attracting others to join in communities and events that address societal, workplace and technological change. With initiatives and events like Corporate Rebels United, Innotribe and Sibos, Peter curates people as his own 'constellation of genius', united by their future focus and creativity. He is particularly drawn to the concept of *scenius* advocated by musician and pro-ducer Brian Eno. In his 2015 BBC Music John Peel Lecture, Eno describes how an exhibition of early twentieth-century Russian artists prompted him to think about the way groups of talented people suddenly come together at a certain time and place. It is a pattern that we can see replicated constantly, from the artists of Renaissance Florence to the Modernists of 1920s Paris, from the punks of 1970s London and New York to the technologists of present-day Silicon Valley. The fragments pull together and movements are born. As Eno explains it, 'genius is the talent of an individual, scenius is the talent of the whole community'.

In *The Power of Pull*, John Hagel, John Seely Brown and Lang Davison offer many other examples of how communities, scenes and industries emerge apparently serendipitously as like-minded individuals find themselves occupying the same spacetime, inevitably learning from and inspiring one another. Yet behind such fortuitous encounters there is often an element of design and infrastructure, whether it is the built environs of cities, the transportation systems or, more recently, internet-enabled platforms like the web and social media. Indy Johar is keenly aware of this. Indy is an architect, institutional designer and co-founder of the strategic design agency 00. Under the aegis of the latter, he has helped establish multiple social ventures, including the Impact Hubs in Westminster and Birmingham. Each has been carefully designed to maximise the effects of interdisciplinary exchange, facilitating the cohabitation and mix of people from different businesses in a fluid and adaptive ecosystem.

The metaobject is a particular area of focus for Indy, that element that creates and implements other objects. This is the role he sees 00 serving, hence its name, suggestive of an administrative system, of the root file path of a computer. 00 is the nucleus around which the many electrons orbit. It has enabled Indy to support a range of experimental initiatives like WikiHouse and Opendesk, as well as the Hub Launchpad open venture accelerator. Through the Dark Matter Laboratories, Indy also aims to apply complex systems science to the resolution of the big issues that confront society, with a particular focus on urban centres and supply chains. How can the apparent problem of borders, boundaries and silos be transformed into an opportunity, into a resource to enable lasting change? This is the fieldwork of the neo-generalist, of the trickster, inspiring others to take action, to engage in research, to develop relevant tools and techniques that have application across different domains.

Indy has lectured widely at academic institutions in the UK, Germany and the USA. He remains a teacher and guide, eager to learn himself even as he advises others. The nine-year-old child who was drawn to reading philosophy, and to the community, discovery and narrative invention of Dungeons and Dragons, still burns brightly within him. Imandeep (Immy) Kaur is someone who has enjoyed a fruitful collaboration with Indy, transitioning from a master–apprentice relationship to one of peers with a shared mission, whether that is through the founding of Birmingham's Impact Hub or the Dark Matters Laboratories or the Town Halls for System Change initiative that is trialling a different form of civic infrastructure. Immy's abilities as convener and producer complement Indy's strategic and leadership experience, their multiple specialisms cohering into a form of collective generalism.

Immy holds a master's degree in International Development but opted early on to apply her array of skills to a youthful and diverse demographic in the Birmingham area, embracing entrepreneurship, inter-faith leadership, social change and think tanks. Her interest in agency and influence applies equally at the level of the individual and that of the city. She recognises that regional cities will need to adopt alternative economic, political and organisational approaches to those followed by the central government. Through her work at the Birmingham Impact Hub, with TEDx and as part of the exploratory 00 projects, she is helping facilitate communities of talent that are open and purpose-driven, bringing together players from the public, private and non-profit sectors. Birmingham is effectively the playground in which this coalition of interested parties experiments and prototypes, seeking out new models and practices that will have enduring societal impact in the twenty-first century. This is adaptive, responsive work countering the tendency towards cultural homogenisation that is the legacy of the Industrial era and old styles of management and civic leadership.

There is something fractal about what Indy and Immy are doing. Everything is designed to scale, the micro reflected in the macro. Each individual element interconnects in service of a larger shared purpose. It is about systems, relationships and meaning. Such integration is known as holonomics, a complete method of interaction, living and working. This is core to how Maria Moraes Robinson experiences her own life and work, and it is the subject of a book she has co-written with her husband Simon Robinson, *Holonomics: Business Where People and Planet Matter*. Their analysis spans systems thinking, mental models, biology, physics, business, economics, spirituality and colour theory, among other topics. Maria's personal experiences growing up in a remote region of Brazil, working in the finance sector, specialising in balanced scorecards, generalising as a consultant, studying in the UK, attending an ashram in India, take shape in a form of mosaic. It is the appreciation of these fragments as the basis of her own identity that has led her to insights about the bigger systems to which we are all integral. The individual, the organisation, the community, the society, the planet, is comprised of many parts but viewed as an organic whole.

Maggie MacDonald is another who has a mosaic-like perspective on who and what she is. Maggie is a non-governmental organisation (NGO) campaigner. She works as an activist with Environmental Defence, an action organisation with a focus on environmental and health issues in Canada. In addition, Maggie is affiliated to the Banff Centre, where she supports the leadership development programme, exploring how people can frame and solve wicked problems using design principles. She also has enjoyed a recording and touring career as a professional musician, and continues her connection to the arts as a novelist, playwright and theatrical performer. Constantly traversing different worlds, Maggie inevitably draws on experiences in one to inform and shape ideas and actions in another, even though she tries to maintain rough boundaries between different aspects of her life. Maggie recognises the contradiction in an apt metaphor, which she uses to help others visualise the multifaceted nature of what she does: she describes herself in terms of the mythological figure of the Chimera, a lion with a goat's head and serpent's tail. For Maggie, the goat represents her omnivorous, wide-ranging curiosity; the lion her fierce advocacy for social justice and loyalty to her community; the snake her artistry and excitement at the prospect of performance.

It is the interaction of these different elements that together contribute to Maggie's sense of identity. The careful equilibrium between each aspect of her personality contributes to her effectiveness in the various fields in which she has chosen to practise. Serial mastery in multiple domains, the ability to shore many fragments, as a boundary-crossing communicator and activist, illustrates the power and value of the neo-generalist. In German, there is a term, *die eierlegende Wollmilchsau*, that is applied in the same dismissive manner as *jack of all trades* in English. It suggests that the person who can fulfil many roles with a high degree of competence is a fantasy figure. Roughly translated as the *egg-laying woolly milk pig*, such a creature would make a fine breakfast for Maggie's impressive Chimera. The neo-generalist gives the lie to those deeply entrenched societal and institutional assumptions about single-track specialism and the deep mining of narrow disciplines. Their success in numerous fields of endeavour prompts others to think differently, looking at the world with fresh eyes.

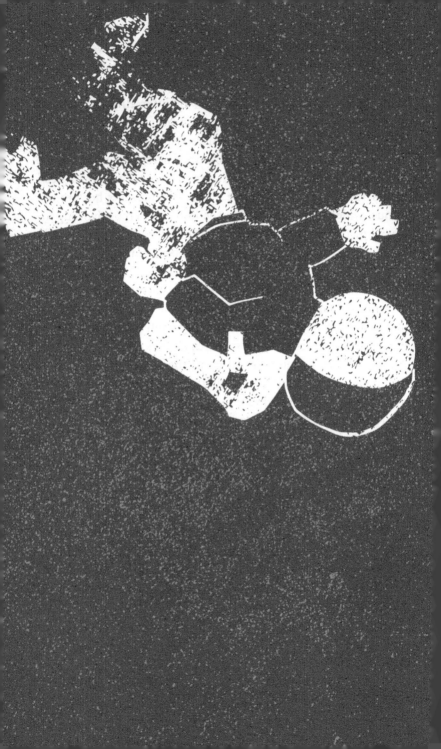

8.
DIVING
BELL

*Something like a giant invisible diving-bell
holds my whole body prisoner ...
My cocoon becomes less oppressive, and
my mind takes flight like a butterfly.*

Jean-Dominique Bauby,
The Diving Bell and the Butterfly

Jean-Dominique Bauby was a journalist and editor of the French fashion magazine *Elle* when he suffered a massive stroke in 1995. The effects were to leave him paralysed in his arms, legs and mouth. Speechless but mentally active, he discovered that the only way he could overcome his locked-in syndrome was to communicate by blinking with his left eye. Hospital staff in Berck-sur-Mer, therapists and visitors would read out letters from a frequency-ordered version of the French alphabet, and Bauby would blink to identify the correct letter, slowly spelling out words, sentences, paragraphs. It was via this method that his memoir, *The Diving Bell and the Butterfly*, was written, appearing in print just two days prior to his death from pneumonia.

Bauby was forced to reframe. He was constrained by the limited view offered by his left eye, by his own diving bell. Mentally he gave expression to the butterfly of memory and interpretation. Through his personal story he also related the stories of his children, partners, carers and an ageing parent. The writing of his book became an exercise in empathy and emotional intelligence between Bauby the patient and whomever happened to be transcribing his words. So too for Bauby the narrator who found the writing process forced him to reassess his personal impact on those around him, placing him in the shoes of other people. It is this ability to reframe, to see problems and opportunities from multiple perspectives, to understand if not agree with different points of view, that is inherent in the neo-generalist. If you live in more than one world, you tend to see in more than one way. It is that chimeric effect that Maggie MacDonald describes.

In Maggie's case, as we have noted, her goat–lion–snake hybrid reflects multiple interests and associated behaviours regarding her border-crossing involvement in artistic performance, community, leadership and social activism. The goat's head symbolises her insatiable curiosity. Ella Saltmarshe also alludes to a goat in her encouragement of polymathic tendencies. Ella argues that the neo-generalist needs to develop remarkable peripheral vision, to be constantly scanning, to have the vision of a goat. Exploring a similar motif, Philip Tetlock and Dan Gardner advocate dragonfly vision in their book *Superforecasting*. The dragonfly's multiple eye lenses pull together a vision of the world around them that is radically different from the binocular perspective of most humans. The notion of reality we construct in our mind's eye is very different from what a goat or dragonfly senses. Is our situational awareness as advanced as theirs? Do we rely too much on external data? Are we inhibited and blinkered by our subjectivity?

Human vision is limited in numerous ways. Whether our eyesight is perfect or corrected with spectacles, context and subjectivity still constrain and shape what we see, filter, process and interpret. With the acquisition of new knowledge, we notice different things or understand the familiar in yet more granular detail. Compare, for example, maps of the Americas as they were first charted in the Tudor era with the maps based on modern-day, satellite-assisted cartography. How much more detail do we have access to today? How much more information is encoded in our digital navigation systems? Scientific discoveries constantly push at the boundaries of what we know, challenging our mindsets, shifting our perspectives. What was accepted fact yesterday, is revealed as misguided error tomorrow. New knowledge is built on the foundations of this revised and edited information. Everything we know is open to challenge and enquiry.

It falls to us to question our own assumptions, to occasionally puncture the bubble of our own realities. One way to do this is to reframe, to frequently adopt the point of view of other people. In 'The Power of Quiet Connectors', Robyn Scott relates the story of a dinner party she co-hosted. As two of the participants were blind, the room in which the dinner took place was completely blacked out. Sighted participants had to adapt, finding themselves at a sensory disadvantage in comparison to their unsighted dinner companions. The result was heightened communication, proper listening, true human engagement. Empathy was an avenue to understanding as personal knowledge was reshaped by shared experience. It is through this form of reframing, or what Philip Weiss refers to as hypershifting, that we gain insights that are so necessary to relationships, creativity and innovation. This behaviour is as vital to the activist as it is to the negotiator, the user experience designer, the counsellor, the traveller, the inventor.

For many years, philosopher Roman Krznaric has explored eclecticism, cultural history and the diversity of perspectives that flow from an empathic mindset. His own curiosity and learning has generated several publications, including *The Wonderbox, How to Find Fulfilling Work* and *Empathy: A Handbook for Revolution*. For Krznaric, empathy is an externally-focused activity that nevertheless has a personal impact. Where introspection is about the self, outrospection is about others. Empathy enables us to gain an understanding of the feelings and points of view of other people, and to then internalise them in order to guide our own actions, engagement with others and creative thinking. It is a case made strongly by singer-songwriter Amanda Palmer who argues in *The Art of Asking* that without empathy there is no possibility either for human understanding or any form of art. It is through empathy that our painters, writers, musicians and filmmakers develop their understanding of the human condition.

These artists tend to be the advance scouts for the rest of us. They tap into, sometimes catalyse, the zeitgeist. They are the tricksters, pushing at the boundaries of the known, crossing borders, experimenting like Picasso, constantly evolving, always becoming. In the digital age, our Twitter and LinkedIn streams are littered with enticements to read the latest pronouncements from the self-titled business gurus and ninjas. Much of what they have to say, however, has been examined in far greater philosophical and compelling depth by the poets, novelists, comedians, cartoonists and television producers of the previous decades. Occasionally, a Peter Drucker or Charles Handy emerges who is a trailblazer, ahead of their time, insightful and illuminating. But such business examples are vanishingly rare. Mark Storm, one of our interviewees, explains that it is his appreciation of art and philosophy that has enabled him to frame better questions. This helps him not just in the workplace but in all facets of his life. Constant questioning can establish empathy. Krznaric has recognised further this powerful association of art and the humanities with empathy via his foundation of the Empathy Library and the Empathy Museum. Through the curation of books, films and personal stories, these collections illustrate the effects of viewing the world with another's eyes.

By way of illustration, consider the popular 1990s television series *Northern Exposure*. It follows the lives and communal interactions of a small group of people living in Cicely, Alaska. The town is the North American equivalent of Macondo, the principal setting of Gabriel García Márquez's classic novel *One Hundred Years of Solitude*. This is neo-modernist television with *Northern Exposure* exploring questions concerning human understanding, relationships, identity, diversity, power and wealth. It is built on the fragmented foundations of cultural allusion, parody and play that inform episode titles, dialogue and plot. The show indulges in extended philosophical musings through the mouthpieces of the ex-con DJ Chris Stevens and his brother Bernard, whose fox-like curiosity and exploration are often in tension with the straightforward, hedgehog-like outlook of businessman and former astronaut Maurice Minnifield.

Audience expectations are confounded on a regular basis through the hybridisation of generic traditions and the collapse of distinctions between East and West, frontier and civilisation, science and magic, male and female, past and present. Like Macondo, Cicely becomes a mythical space; a repository of all human experiences, philosophies and civilisations. This is a location where different cultures, religions, ideologies, even psychic spaces become shared. Cicely is where temporal, spatial and personal divisions can be elided. The eternal present reigns, and the discovery of Napoleonic warriors and mammoths, visitations from ghosts and characters sharing or exchanging dreams are treated as commonplace.

Northern Exposure creates a magical-realist universe in which the fantastic and the commonplace are treated equally. The daily activities of Joel Fleischman, Chris, Maggie O'Connell, Ruth-Anne Miller and Holling Vincoeur, catering to their community as doctor, DJ, pilot, general store owner and bar proprietor, respectively, are juxtaposed with explorations of ritual, shamanism and dreamworlds. Mythology and its association with journeys to self-understanding is ever-present. The work of Joseph Campbell and Jean Shinoda Bolen is overtly referenced, while narrative structure is occasionally informed by the former's monomyth. It serves as the model for 'The Quest', one of the key episodes of the final season. Here Joel and Maggie seek out the Jewelled City of the North, culminating with Joel's return to New York City, his personal grail ever since he was first posted to the remote Alaskan outpost of Cicely in the series' pilot episode.

Often the Native American characters become associated with the fantastic. The differences between their worldview and that of city characters like Joel is eloquently suggested, for example, in their alternative approaches to medicine. Science is juxtaposed with magic, usually to comic effect. It is the industrial world and its practices butting up against traditions drawn from nomadic and agricultural lifestyles. Marilyn Whirlwind fulfils the trickster role here, serving as the conduit between two worldviews, two mindsets. The fantastic, however, is not the exclusive domain of the Native Americans. Chris, for one, actively seeks out such experiences, and they also become part of life in Cicely for many of the other characters. Ed Chigliak, for example, is hounded by a demon figure known as the Green Man whenever he encounters self-doubt. Many of the town's inhabitants are constantly dreaming, blurring fantasy and reality, even experiencing one another's mindscreens, as in 'Aurora Borealis: A Fairy Tale for Grown-Ups'. Fantastic communal events also occur with regularity. In 'Horns', for example, bottled Cicely water has the effect of reversing gender behaviour in the town.

One of the most fascinating things about *Northern Exposure* is its portrait of community, its advocacy of connection and communication. Cicely is a small town that celebrates the multidimensional, that welcomes in, adapts to and absorbs outsiders like Joel, Chris, Shelly Tambo or Mike Monroe. It is a network with hubs centred around the bar, grocery store, radio studio and medical practice. Through its empathic presentation of similarity and difference, the show examines a spectrum of mindsets, ideologies, cultural practices, ethnicities and stereotypes relating to gender and sexual orientation. The humorous counterpoint of science and magic, idealism and reality, capitalism and counterculture, past and present, native and visitor, prompts regular shifts in perspective and understanding, not only by the characters within the story's frame but by the viewers too. In this sense, *Northern Exposure* blends entertainment with education. It is a study in and appreciation of humanity in all its glorious Technicolor.

The celebration of human diversity and meaningful connection is a quality shared by Ed Brenegar. If he were to sketch out his own chimera, it would reflect his varied experiences as a Presbyterian minister, leadership consultant, traveller and change agent. Ed has a broad academic background, having opted to major in American Studies, drawn to its interdisciplinarity rather than the pursuit of a single specialism. This he has supplemented through an ongoing personal interest in history and philosophy, further education at a seminary, experiences as minister and chaplain, facilitation of education programmes and work in the business sector. In many respects, Ed is a Christian humanist; his faith a lens through which he appreciates fellow humans and seeks to understand how he can assist them in fulfilling their potential. In the context of the Church, he is something of a misfit, a non-religious minister disinterested in dogma or in fulfilling the role of 'curator for the museum of memories'.

In thought and deed, Ed is a frequent border-crosser. 'Everywhere I go is home,' he observes. His interest in human relationships overrides superficial signifiers of difference such as language, faith or ethnicity. Ed demonstrates a cultural flexibility, adapting to context. A defining experience was when he spent time supporting refugees at a camp in Pakistan during the Soviet–Afghan War. When you open yourself to other ways of life, other worlds, it gives you a different perspective on your homeland and on what preoccupies people there. Currently based in Jackson, Wyoming, Ed both belongs and is an outsider, experiencing the fluctuating status of the trickster and neo-generalist. Extensive travels and temporary residencies in the many states of his own immense country, as well as numerous ventures to foreign lands, have exposed him regularly to similarities and differences, to a variety of overlapping and contrasting worldviews and mindsets, to his own form of dragonfly vision. This has been a source of insight and the catalyst for change agency. The view from the edge is very different from that at the centre.

Ed relates a story from his time in Oklahoma that illustrates the different ways people see and think. In the early 1960s, the Church had determined to build an education centre but the congregation was divided on whether to construct a one- or two-storey edifice. Eventually a compromise was reached whereby a second floor was built but was left unfinished until required. Some quarter of a century later, during the period of Ed's involvement, still with an unfinished top floor, the Church leaders reflected back on this as a golden moment in the community and its shared history. For Ed, looking on with the perspective of an outsider, he could only see a catastrophic failure, a missed opportunity to effectively serve the local people, reeling off the many different ways in which a fully finished education centre could have been used.

Where the Church sought validation of past actions, Ed wished to disabuse them of their confirmation bias. He could offer different domain knowledge, a different point of view, an alternative reality. His situational awareness, his ability to identify and synthesise critical information, led him to a more rounded perspective regarding the history of the education centre. But what he was confronted with was the myopia of the local expert. A timeless fable that, with minor variations, could occur in any place. Indeed, there is always the danger, in a specialist world, that we get stuck in the furrows we have ploughed. Digging ever deeper, we fail to pause to scan the skies or peer over the ridge of the trench. We lose context, forgetting the overall geography of the field in which we stand. Our connection to the surrounding region therefore breaks down. We construct our own localised, closed system. Until entropy inevitably has its way. Our system then fails, our specialism suddenly rendered redundant. The expertise we valued so highly has served to narrow and shorten our vision. It has blinded us to potential and opportunity.

The Oklahoman experience highlighted for Ed the challenges of working within the institution of the Church, where the minister is expected to maintain the status quo rather than debunk it, to honour history and tradition rather than co-create a new narrative. Moving away from ministry and into leadership education and consultancy proved a better fit with his notion of service, continuous learning and transformation. Ed's personal story is filled with examples of guidance and mentoring. Like Brian Grazer, the Hollywood producer and co-author of *A Curious Mind*, Ed pursues an emotional curiosity. He favours a conversational, interactive approach. Ed is constantly reframing from the perspective of others, pursuing Socratic enquiry, connecting people and ideas, contextualising fragments in terms of the whole, all with the intention of helping individuals and organisations realise their ideas and fulfil their desired change. Empathy is Ed's path to actualisation both of the self and of the collective. Communication is a method both to understand and to be understood.

Ed's story demonstrates the values of leaving the doors and windows open, allowing in external influences, alternative perspectives. Regardless of context or sector, these can energise, sustain and help engender new practice and behaviour. Some inspirational examples regarding receptiveness and openness to alternative methods and ideas have come from healthcare. They include the pioneering German surgeons who recognised the scientific nature of medical practice, and understood the need for sterility symbolised by the white laboratory coats they opted to wear. They also include the joint endeavours of the Great Ormond Street Hospital surgical team and the Ferrari Formula 1 pit-stop team who partnered together to improve the hospital's post-surgery handover procedures. Then there is the account, recorded by Atul Gawande in *The Checklist Manifesto*, of medical staff seeking to reduce the incidence of post-surgical infection by learning lessons from the aviation, construction and finance industries. All are examples where highly skilled individuals, however temporarily, removed the blinkers of their expertise, opening themselves to the ideas and points of view of other people, other walks of life.

Examples of positive deviance highlight situations where experts have chosen to put their own knowledge and experience on hold. Instead, they have elected to learn from emergent practices demonstrated by community members who have diverged from or modified standardised behaviours. The aim is not to impose or blend outside knowledge, as was the case with Great Ormond Street and Ferrari, but to amplify what already exists within the community. To uncover and broadcast it for the benefit of all. The outsider here has a catalytic effect. The experiences of Jerry and Monique Sternin working on behalf of Save the Children in Vietnam is a case in point. Tasked with addressing child malnutrition in a short time frame, the Sternins opted to observe both common and deviant practice. They learned that the healthier children tended to be members of families that provided smaller but more frequent meals than was the norm. In addition, these families tended to add other ingredients to their traditional rice dishes. Dependent on where they lived, this might include shrimps, crabs, snails, sweet-potato greens, peanuts and sesame seeds. Sources of protein and vitamins to supplement the children's intake of carbohydrates.

The encouraging results of these practices were shared widely. Positively deviant parents explained to others how they had added variety to their children's meals, leading to broader adoption and ongoing experimentation. Not only individuals but entire villages learned from one another. They were exposed to different practices, internalised them and adapted them to suit their own context. The solution to child malnutrition was personalised, home-made, evolutionary and communal. It emerged from within rather than being imposed from the realm of the alien expert briefly parachuted in to espouse a colour-by-numbers quick fix. The positive deviant took on the role of guide. Local networks, reframing and fox-like curiosity trumped the one right way of the hedgehog. A biological analogy shared with us by Susy Paisley-Day is illuminating: viewed as organisms, these communities demonstrated a form of phenotypic plasticity, transforming diet and behaviour in order to ensure survival. Economically and environmentally constrained, they had to adapt and respond to context.

Another biological allusion has relevance to James Tyer's experience working for a multinational food manufacturer. James is a learning strategy consultant, but has also fulfilled a role while based in Canada and the UK as the global lead on social collaboration for the multinational. From his outsider-on-the-inside perspective, the picture he paints of this venerable institution is one of stasis, rigid hierarchy and resistance to change. In their work on evolutionary biology during the 1970s, Stephen Jay Gould and Niles Eldredge developed the concept of punctuated equilibrium. Their theory proposes that species evidence minimal evolutionary change over millions of years, which explains why there is so little fossilised record of transformation. Instead fossils taken from different eras indicate relative stability. When evolutionary transformation happens, it takes place very quickly and at the edges of the population, usually in isolation, before a new period of equilibrium ensues. The process is staccato rather elongated and gradual.

For James, he was confronted with an established population that he had to seek to transform, catalysing a period of rapid change centred on adaptation to the digital workplace. James had to gain an understanding of his new environment and those he worked with. To achieve this, it was necessary for him to exercise his own curiosity, while also drawing on his knowledge of psychology and sociology. Educated in political sciences, James has gravitated towards the kind of roles that enable him to continue learning, while serving as connector, facilitator, translator and community manager. His interest is in networks, nurturing the relationships they enable, while bridging between specialisms, opening the doors between different silos, allowing ideas and information to flow.

The neo-generalist, James believes, is always learning what is next rather than what is official or set. He understands that it will often fall to him to lead the way to that next thing, challenging the established order, helping others to see and think differently. With his sojourn at the food manufacturer, however, it remained unclear whether he would enjoy success in establishing a new mindset, instilling the kind of responsiveness that is necessary to cope with the digitally-enabled challenges and needs of the twenty-first century. He was finding too few rebels to join his cause. As with Ed before him, he encountered people who preferred living in a museum to any form of transformation, languishing in a culture characterised by the expectation of deference rather than earned respect. Better the stale air they knew than the freshening winds of change.

Another metaphor serves James well: that of the bridge. With a bridge either/or is replaced by both/and. With a bridge, it is no longer a case of here or there but here *and* there. Not in or out but in *and* out. Not us or them but us *and* them. Not past or present but past *and* present *and* future too. In professional cycling, a rider bridges the gap when they ride off the front of the peloton and catch up with the breakaway. They bridge across through both space and time. When they make their move, they are simultaneously part of the peloton and part of the breakaway. They are in both places and in no place. Numerous bridges have spanned the River Thames, the older ones built with the benefit of diving bells that supplied air to the crews working below the water's surface. Standing on a London bridge, you are both on the North Bank and the South Bank and in neither place. In another variant of the diving bell, the astronauts on the International Space Station are both of the Earth and outside it, seeing their home planet in a completely new way. The bridge is an invitation to exploration.

With the digital bridge represented by the hyperlink, you can be both within and outside your organisation. For James, mostly working remotely from the multinational's US headquarters, such a digital bridge provides succour, enabling access to a global network, alternative ideas, learning opportunities, inspiration and support. In Philip Pullman's *His Dark Materials* trilogy, the young trickster protagonists are able to cut doorways allowing them to move back and forth between different worlds, different dimensions. The digital bridge of social media and the smartphone app fulfils a similar function, providing temporary respite from the rigidity of organisational cultures, rules and regulations. It is the conduit via which the neo-generalist can bring together multiple disciplines, to introduce and reframe from external perspectives, questioning preconceptions, encouraging openness of mind and receptiveness to the other. In focusing on an enterprise social network, James is taking small steps that he hopes will make at least a handful of his colleagues see, connect and communicate in new ways. A little rebellion at the edges may foment rapid transformation.

A vocabulary takes shape from these accumulated stories. It embraces the outsider, the misfit, the rebel, deviancy, dissent, critique, activism and change agency. People like Roman Krznaric, the characters of *Northern Exposure*, the Vietnamese villagers, Maggie, Mark, Ella, Ed and James all ask *What if? Is this right? Might there be another way? How can we improve things?* It is this sort of challenging, inquisitive mindset that was celebrated in Apple's *Think Different* marketing campaign, launched after Steve Jobs resumed his leadership of the company in 1997: 'Here's to the crazy ones. The misfits. The rebels. The troublemakers. The round pegs in the square holes. The ones who see things differently. They're not fond of rules. And they have no respect for the status quo. You can quote them, disagree with them, glorify or vilify them. But the only thing you can't do is ignore them. Because they change things. They push the human race forward. While some may see them as the crazy ones, we see genius. Because the people who are crazy enough to think they can change the world, are the ones who do.'

Apple's television campaign included advertisements featuring some of the iconic figures of the last century, including Einstein, Picasso, Martha Graham, Martin Luther King and Thomas Edison.

Individuals celebrated for their difference, inspiration and innovation. Sarah Miller Caldicott is an author and innovation consultant who just happens to be Edison's great-grandniece. The breadth of her advisory experiences has resulted in a broad, generalist expertise on innovation and entrepreneurialism. This is supplemented by a business school education and work in marketing, product development and brand management. It services her specialism on Edison and his working practices, reflected in such publications as *Innovate Like Edison* and *Midnight Lunch*. Sarah frequently finds herself having to reframe from her ancestor's perspective in order to gain understanding of innovation, creativity, collaboration and workforce diversity.

Edison's inventions had a huge impact on household lighting, cinema, sound recording and communication technologies. But even with the move towards mass production and the co-founding of General Electric, he demonstrated a belief in bringing generalists and specialists together in his teams, where he expressed an interest as much in the individual as in the collective and the process. For Edison, there was a complementarity in the way generalists and specialists looked at problems and opportunities, how they recognised different patterns and were able to communicate what they saw. Collectively they had the dragonfly vision that could see the way to a new invention. It was generalists and specialists together, not solitary hyperspecialists, who helped create the mystique that surrounded the research activities at Edison's laboratory in Menlo Park. This was a place of constant experimentation and learning, new inventions resulting from the exhaustive exploration of all alternatives, as well as creative hybridisation.

Sarah herself is an accomplished pianist, also studying harpsichord while at college. Here too, with music, it is noteworthy how she puts herself in the shoes of past masters, adopting an analytical approach as both listener and performer, seeking to understand how pieces should be played as intended by the composer.

In *Creative Confidence*, David and Tom Kelley observe that to build on the ideas of others requires humility, an acknowledgement that you do not have all the answers. We all stand on the shoulders of giants, borrowing from and adapting what came before. We attempt to fuse our own perspective with that of another. As an adviser on innovation, Sarah uses the lessons and methods of the past to establish a scaffolding for the future. She has learned from Edison the art of consistently questioning everything, of the cross-pollination of projects and ideas, and of the blending that can result from multidisciplinarity, scanning the peripheries for opportunities to learn and innovate whether in the arts, utilities, healthcare or horticulture.

The innovative mindset can result in the creation of new products, in new forms of connection and communication. This was Edison's legacy. Sometimes, however, it services the reinvention of the self, the move towards a new identity, a new way of looking at the world and our place in it. As with so many of our neo-generalist interviewees, Scott Torrance was someone who constantly sought to avoid labels, only recently self-selecting that of illustrator. Scott's ambition and curiosity resulted in a breadth of knowledge and a frenetic pace of life. He was a butterfly, relentlessly exploring and learning, a high-flyer at a variety of corporate roles in the retail and IT sales sectors, before moving into business consultancy and establishing his own content marketing agency. He was prevalent on social media too, an early adopter of new services like Twitter, Instagram and Periscope, active in many networks, connecting people, sharing ideas, nurturing relationships, leading and guiding. Yet he suddenly found himself compelled to withdraw and redefine himself.

Scott's body had ceased functioning in the way he wanted it to. His personal diving bell took the form of Elhers Danlos Syndrome-Hypermobility Type. It affected mobility, posture and vision, inducing both chronic pain and fatigue. Scott had to stop everything. He withdrew into the controlled environment of home, put work on hold, gave up social media and started to relearn how to use his muscles, how to sit, how to hold his head, how to move. With only a few waking hours available to him each day, and much of that time given over to therapeutic exercise and recovery, Scott's focus now was on the two things most important to him: his family and drawing. When he spoke to us, Scott was still processing the changes in his life, but already he was conveying a strong sense of someone who had reframed, shedding an old identity and stepping into a new one.

Visual thinking had become increasingly important to Scott while still in consultancy, prompting his decision to start up the content marketing agency. Drawing now has become central to his life, defining who he is as an illustrator, assisting his rehabilitation process, and allowing the flights of his imagination to manifest themselves on the page, even if he is unable to remove himself very often from the protective environment of home. Drawing has given him a new way of seeing and interpreting the world, of communicating with others. It energises him; a source of passion and motivation. Scott speaks now of dedicating himself to multiple forms of visual art: to illustration, children's books, comics and gallery installations that capture the swirling kaleidoscope of his mind.

Scott has realised that for him it is art rather than social media that has become the bridge through which he connects to others and continues to learn. He invites other people to see as he does. He has discovered that even through the mind's eye and the hand's movement, where you go is who you are. In looking for meaning, researching and adapting to his new condition, Scott has discovered who he is.

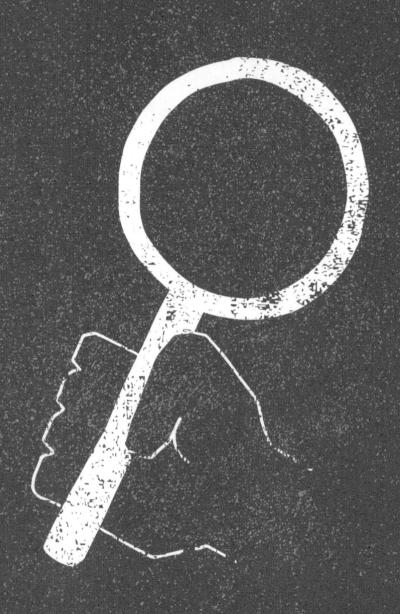

9.
LOT 49

*A revelation also trembled just past
the threshold of her understanding.*

Thomas Pynchon, *The Crying of Lot 49*

It is the lot of meaning-makers and inquisitive sense-makers to while away the hours sifting through the detritus and effluent of mankind and its fellow species on the planet. In *Underworld*, his contribution to the tradition of the Great American Novel, Don DeLillo writes about the life and times of Nick Shay, a waste management executive, embracing the spectrum from the disposal of household litter to the management of toxic nuclear matter. It includes a paean to Staten Island's vast Fresh Kills landfill site. This is a setting apparently revisited by Maxine Tarnow in Thomas Pynchon's *Bleeding Edge*, a contemporary detective novel that explores a world shaped in equal measure by the internet and terrorism. In Pynchon's earlier *The Crying of Lot 49*, a novelistic reworking of T. S. Eliot's *The Waste Land*, he has his accidental detective, Oedipa Maas, bump up against the machinations of the mysterious W.A.S.T.E.

Beyond the imagination of our great wordsmiths, painter Chris Ofili has incorporated elephant droppings into works of art that explore his understanding of the human condition. Others have fused environmental concern, craft and commerce, recycling old plumbing materials, damaged street railings and disused car parts, to create decorative artefacts and household lighting. In the city of York, archaeologists have examined fossilised human excrement as a means of expanding our knowledge about diet, state of health, agriculture and trade during the period of Viking occupancy of the northeast of England. Similarly, in South America, conservation biologist and artist Susy Paisley-Day has depended on the careful examination of animal waste to help unlock secrets about a resident species.

Now an Honorary Research Fellow of the University of Kent, Susy began her association with the Durrell Institute of Conservation and Ecology (DICE) in the mid-1990s while carrying out PhD research studying the spectacled bear and its relationship with the people of Bolivia. One of the objectives of her research was the first radio-telemetry study of wild bears. This involved overcoming the constraints of academic sponsorship and the misplaced good intentions of key decision-makers who feared for the well-being of a young woman trekking into the rugged landscape of the Apolobamba region of the Andes, where she hoped to radio-collar the bears, enabling a longer term survey of the species.

Susy's detective journey, then, began on the valley floor with the analysis of bear waste. Although the spectacled bear eats animal prey and carrion, it is among the more herbivorous of bear species; what Susy refers to as an 'opportunistic omnivore'. Its waste, therefore, serves as a rich source of data. When this is combined with knowledge of where certain wild berries, cultivated plants and tropical vegetation grow, it can indicate where the bears might be found. An appreciation of what the bears were eating ultimately led to higher ground. It was a case of seeking signs, looking for scratch markings, developing search images, scanning for food sources and waiting patiently for the bears to visit them. Expertise in bears, their habitats and behaviours was important in helping decipher clues and recognise patterns. So too an empathy for and affinity with the local people, and an evolving appreciation of the environment and the indigenous populations' function within it.

From the perspective of neo-generalism, these detective traits, particularly as they apply to sense-making and pattern recognition, are where the logic of the scientist is hybridised with the wandering of the flâneur. The acquisition and application of knowledge is juxtaposed with mystery, uncertainty and ambiguity. Susy was able to utilise these broad capabilities to bridge from the known to the unknown, to track and collar her prey, and expand what we know about the spectacled bear. By carefully reading and assessing clues, she was able to solve a puzzle. Signs were read and decoded, narratives constructed as a consequence, decisions and actions then taken.

In other situations, however, it is wise to be cautious about the identification of patterns. We tend to be sensitive to and recognise signs that fit with our current interests and preoccupations, filtering out everything that does not. Pattern recognition, therefore, requires a fine balancing act between perception and reality; an awareness that the objective can be affected and distorted by the subjective. Confirmation bias is to be avoided. We can all fall into the trap of wilful blindness. Our popular culture is filled with the detectives of literary fiction, cinema and television who write or talk themselves into meaning and understanding as they decipher the clues and signs that surround them. Often, however, there is a disjuncture between the signifier and the signified. Perception and reality diverge. Many of these detectives – Jake Gittes in *Chinatown*, Leonard Shelby in *Memento*, Maude in *Elizabeth is Missing*, the drug-addled protagonists of *The Big Lebowski* and *Inherent Vice* – suffer from sensory impairment, memory loss or cognitive difficulties.

In the case of Oedipa Maas, she may well have stumbled upon the sinister activities of Trystero, or it is possible that its ubiquitous muted horn symbol could simply be an externalisation of her own mounting paranoia; a misreading of signs, a misrecognition of patterns, the pitfalls of apophenia. Henry Doss, reflecting on his experiences teaching English literature, asks whether Oedipa decodes or encodes? Is she discovering or creating as her investigative adventure leads her full circle back to the book's title? Where *The Crying of Lot 49* closes on those same words, Eliot's *The Waste Land* leads the reader to the *word* with which the appended and carefully crafted notes close. The poem is about literature itself; a view of the world and mankind's journey through it that is filtered via the assembly of fragments from a multitude of other literary sources. In one sense, then, these adventures offer nothing but the signifiers from which they are formed.

This self-reflexivity is an important ingredient in the detective's tale. It is the figure of 'Paul Auster', for example, who becomes central to Paul Auster's novella *City of Glass*. The inner doll in a series of Russian dolls. Detectives create through their actions, shape through their narration. They seek meaning, but often they are themselves entangled in what they investigate. They head out on a quest and find themselves in the middle of the labyrinth. The knowledge they acquire teaches them much, not only about the world around them, but about themselves too. Their hero adventure leads to self-understanding and self-actualisation. As E. E. Cummings phrases it, 'it's always ourselves we find in the sea'.

The tradition can be traced back at least to Oedipa's namesake in Sophocles's trilogy of Theban plays, becoming entangled with Freudianism and other psychoanalytical schools of thought that linger at the edges of cultural production and analysis. Oedipus, the Theban monarch who solves the Sphinx's riddle, was one of the first detectives to feature in Western culture. However, in unravelling the mystery of his own life, he comes to realise that he murdered his own father and married his mother, the discovery of which prompts her suicide. His response is to blind himself in both eyes. The story establishes a number of themes which resurface in the detective stories that have become so familiar to us in the last two centuries. Tales of detection play with our assumptions about logic, deduction and sense-making. They both build up and debunk the notion of the solitary, heroic figure making meaning out of chaos.

Such narratives also riff on ideas about the senses, especially vision and, by extension, insight. Examples include Oedipus's blindness, Alex Cutter's eye patch in *Cutter's Way* or Brother William's use of glasses in *The Name of the Rose*. They are stories that are as much about the detectives themselves as the mysteries they investigate. First-person narration, voice-over commentary and flashbacks are common, serving to fragment the story, eliding temporal and spatial divisions, while also establishing a subjective point of view, regardless of whether this is trustworthy or not. The protagonists are frequently co-creators of the sequence of events that unfold, implicated themselves by what they discover. Their telephoto lenses slowly bringing into focus either their own criminality, as in the case of Oedipus's patricide and incest, or their leading role in the machinations of a criminal figure. Think Holmes and Moriarty in Conan Doyle's writing; Sam Spade and Brigid O'Shaughnessy in *The Maltese Falcon*; Martin Rohde and Sebastian Sandstrod in *The Bridge*.

It is intriguing that during the industrial era, different detective types emerged in our popular culture. On the one hand, we have the flâneur of Honoré de Balzac and Charles Baudelaire. This is the dilettante street-walker and observer of people, who will evolve into the hardboiled gumshoe of the twentieth century, epitomised by Dashiell Hammett's Sam Spade and Raymond Chandler's Philip Marlowe. By contrast, there is the cold, logical, almost machine-like figure of the ratiocinative tradition: characters like Edgar Allan Poe's Auguste Dupin, Conan Doyle's Sherlock Holmes and Agatha Christie's Miss Marple and Hercule Poirot. Police procedurals, featuring characters like Georges Simenon's Jules Maigret, belong more to a tradition of intuitive detection. Here too, then, there is a spectrum of approaches. What is intriguing is how these become hybridised in *Sherlock*, the BBC modernisation of Doyle's creation, written by Mark Gatiss and Steven Moffat.

This version of Holmes is a complex figure who, like a neo-generalist, appears to switch in and out of different roles, different personae, even different time periods in the case of the 2016 broadcast, 'The Abominable Bride'. When he succumbs to the ratiocinative mode, he is dehumanised, veering towards the extremes of science and logic, the pursuit of a single, right answer.

At such times, he becomes a pawn in the games being played by Moriarty and Magnussen. He fails to see the big picture, fails to recognise that he is both subject and object of a grander scheme. It is a flaw of the binary world. What if the world cannot be explained away in ones and zeroes? What if there are many shades of grey rather than just black and white? What if the patterns we sense and follow are just one option among many? What if we all perceive different patterns? The ratiocinative Sherlock's great shortcoming is his lack of empathy for others. It prevents him from reframing and seeing things from the perspective of other people. Instead everything remains theoretical, a puzzle to be solved.

We are given a glimpse of a different aspect of Holmes, though. This is the hardboiled figure who can mobilise street people or hide in a drugs den. This kind of detective usually lives on the edge of society, which allows them to bridge between different social strata. They are connectors, moving fluidly through their network, from edge to centre, from centre to edge. They ask questions, converse and observe. The gumshoe's actions catalyse events. Their quiet periods of observation, walking the streets, sitting in cars, listening to wiretaps, looking through cameras and binoculars, allow certain elements to emerge from the chaos. When Holmes fulfils this role he becomes more empathetic, more willing, for example, to rescue Irene Adler when her life is in danger, or to take radical action in dealing with Mary Watson's persecutor.

The twenty-first-century Holmes, then, blends aspects of the traditional ratiocinative detective with those of the hardboiled gumshoe. He is a trickster, living in and navigating his way through many worlds, including those of the homeless, the criminal underworld, the police, the media and the civil service. He translates information into the language of each world. At one moment he appears nothing more than a human extension of his smartphone or laptop, surfing the binary code of the digital domain. In the next he is servicing the flesh-and-blood needs of a junkie aficionado of classical music. Like a computer he needs data to process, whether gathered from interviews, forensic analysis or conversation with Watson. But he is also someone who requires time for reflection in order to sensemake, interpret patterns and construct narratives. Technology is an enabler that frees rather than inhibits his cognitive capabilities. His mind palace is but a metaphor for his sifting and filtering of information and its translation into actionable knowledge.

Conan Doyle's ability as a writer of detective fiction was indebted to his own medical training. In *A Muse and A Maze*, Peter Turchi draws parallels between the forensic activities and information gathering of the detective and the medical professional's interviewing of patients and analysis of test results. Both the doctor and the detective collect data, shape it into meaningful narratives and arrive at conclusions that result in the diagnosis and treatment of a patient or the arrest and prosecution of a criminal. In the Holmes stories, Watson stands in as a surrogate for the author, intimately involved in events, benefiting from his military and medical experience, and serving as narrator. It is Watson who acts as meaning-maker for the benefit of the reader, filtering and shaping from his own perspective, assembling clues and events into a coherent narrative, contextualising. He narrates retrospectively, already aware of how the mystery portrayed unravels, serving as guide and educator as he gradually reassembles the story pieces.

The art of storytelling, the ability to sift information and data, to forage and curate people and ideas, to repackage them into meaningful narratives that can guide, assist and influence others is a key attribute of the neo-generalist. It is exposure to and mastery of multiple disciplines that enhances this capability, enabling communication and storytelling that transcends boundaries; that can be received and understood by diverse audiences.

It helps bridge the gaps between different areas of expertise, exposing ideas from one silo in a new context that can infect decision-making, problem-solving and opportunity-making in another silo. It informs and influences different communities to take action, often in cooperation with one another. This is as relevant to a medical practitioner like Tara Swart as it is to a brand specialist like Marvin Abrinica, as useful to an environmental campaigner like Maggie MacDonald as to a writer like Dolly Garland, as essential to a scientist like Susy Paisley-Day as to a business consultant like Simon Terry.

Simon, for example, explains that his passion for poetry, its distillation of the human experience, has taught him how to help clients identify and communicate their sense of purpose, to understand the contexts within which they find themselves and to identify appropriate solutions. Marvin, a former student of English Literature, draws on his understanding of story structure and archetypes to help organisations develop their brands, their sense of identity and a corporate narrative that extends from the past into the future. His own pattern recognition capabilities stem from his role as a connector of disciplines, people and ideas. He is the bridge between and curator of different PhD specialists. Before pursuing work in conservation biology, and her own PhD, Susy also benefitted from a liberal arts education. This gave her another lens with which to approach science; a generalist foundation, both artistic and humanist, that enriched her specialism. In a typical jump on the specialist–generalist continuum, it is her science now that feeds her art and the stories she tells.

For Susy, the self-reflexive physical tracking of a bear in order to electronically track a bear opens up a wider narrative. This is about understanding different actors and systems that cohere into an overarching ecosystem. It includes an appreciation of ecological niches, of the careful equilibrium and interdependency of flora and fauna, of the relationship between human inhabitants and the bears in the region she explored. This extends into an anthropological interpretation of bear mythology and costume in the Andes. The knowledge and information acquired about diversity, balance and potential harm during this academic research has been crafted not only into a PhD thesis and journal articles, but also informs Susy's work in social enterprise and as a textile designer. Her visual art continues to tell stories about the conservation of ecosystems and the protection of endangered species. They represent a powerful fusion of her scientific expertise and storytelling capabilities; artefacts that can simultaneously delight, educate and influence. They draw on deep knowledge acquired in one discipline translating it into the language of another. This is underpinned by an ongoing connection to, understanding of and relationship with the people of the regions she seeks to support with her work.

The sharing of a narrative, regardless of the medium within which it is packaged, is the ultimate goal of detection. Whether the detective figure is a policeman, journalist, scientist, artist, lecturer, doctor or lawyer, a story offers the opportunity to share a personal perspective, to navigate through chaos, to impart knowledge, to influence and inspire. Harold Jarche describes personal knowledge mastery as three interdependent processes. It begins with seeking. The detective gathers clues and facts. They read and observe, leverage their network, talk with people, ask questions, walk the streets and the digital airwaves. The second stage is sense-making. The detective reviews and assesses. They seek out patterns, synergies and anomalies. They synthesise different information sources, internalising them, making them their own. They look at what they have from different perspectives. They begin to craft a meaningful narrative, which inevitably contains a part of themselves and their own worldview. The final stage is sharing. The detective presents what they have learned in a form that can be consumed and acted upon by others. They narrate their work. They work out loud. What is shared generates further learning, contextual critique and feedback. The cycle starts over again, leading to further refinement and new insight.

In Orson Welles's celebrated film *Citizen Kane*, an early sequence features a newsreel that offers a superficial canter through the life of Charles Foster Kane. The investigative reporter responsible for it is tasked with going deeper, seeking out an interpretation of the last word Kane uttered before his death: *Rosebud*. What follows is personal knowledge mastery in action: the detective figure assembling and sifting through multiple perspectives of one man's life, gaining access to a diversity of information sources and the recollections of people who had either personal or professional relationships with Kane. Both structure and narrative are fragmented as the reporter–detective pursues different lines of enquiry. The film closes with him still stuck at the sense-making stage while the viewer is supplied with a missing element that allows them to complete their own interpretation. Kane's palatial home has been transformed temporarily into an immense warehouse after his death. Among the thousands of artefacts that he has accumulated – the fragments shoring up his own ruins – we are shown his childhood sledge bearing the name Rosebud. A signifier of lost youth and innocence that overlays all that has gone before with a shroud of regret.

The reporter's task in *Citizen Kane* is to synthesise these different points of view into a single narrative that would have meaning for any one of his interviewees, or for someone entirely new to Kane's story. This becomes the film itself, which in narrative terms, therefore, is left incomplete; a loose assembly of pieces. Only the viewer is able to solve the film's puzzle and even then – given personal and subjective preferences, context and areas of focus – the picture portrayed from one viewer to the next is likely to diverge in important ways. The film reflects the difficulties of communication, of repackaging what we know for the benefit of others. This lies at the heart of storytelling as a form of engagement. Is it possible to ensure that our intended meaning is verbalised, conveyed textually or condensed into a visual metaphor as simple and powerful as the image of a burning sledge? How, for example, do people like Susy, Maggie MacDonald, Bill Liao, Robin Chase and Lucian Tarnowski find ways to communicate everything they know about conservation, environmental preservation, global warming and water security so that it both educates and moves people to action?

Stories themselves conform to patterns. They are comprised of certain structures, archetypes, forms, containers and presentational techniques. They bear both similarities and differences determined by context and discipline. An academic paper, for example, is very different from a newspaper article covering the same topic. This in turn has little in common with a narrative poem, which itself bears scant resemblance to a tapestry, which is distinct from a stand-up comedian's carefully crafted joke, which contrasts with the lyrics of a folk song. The neo-generalist, then, not only has to be able to detect patterns and make sense of them, but they themselves need to find meaningful ways to relate acquired knowledge and ideas through stories-as-patterns. These can often be micro narratives that convey big ideas. A fragment that elucidates a system.

Briony Marshall is a sculptor and installation artist who trained as a biochemist. Her artworks reflect her understanding of human society as a form of organism. To understand ourselves, we have to understand our component parts at a fractal level. We are DNA, chemicals, enzymes, molecules, carbon. We undergo genesis and growth, from fertilised embryo to foetus, passing through the Carnegie stages, emerging as infant human beings, transforming into social creatures. As with the bears that Susy tracked in Bolivia, we adapt to our habitats, shaped by both culture and ecosystem. Briony's work tells stories of humans crafting their own worlds, their own networks, on top of the natural world. Of borders and edges between different worlds that require trickster figures to traverse them. Of a particular form of pattern recognition, divination and interpretation that has infused different stages of human organisation in the form of shamanism and chiromancy. These stories, these ideas, add rich layers of meaning to her complex sculptures.

For Briony, art entices people in because of its beauty and its narrative. It is a form of engagement that enables understanding about topics people have never even thought about in detail before. As someone who herself crosses borders between science, medicine and art, she draws on her neo-generalism to enable change in others. This can result from the catalytic effect of bringing different worldviews, different mindsets, together. Or it can be the innovative impact of her own work combining contrasting disciplines and ideas in new and creative ways. In making her art she simultaneously learns and educates. Living in several worlds, she is particularly sensitive to patterns. Turchi argues that patterns create anticipation. Briony extends this to process, which she interprets as a form of pattern. Drawing parallels between processes across her experiences in education, business, science and art has resulted in personal insight, transformation and creativity. This manifests itself in an understanding not only of human society as an organism but of the fact that, from a systems thinking perspective, everything connects.

An appreciation of the interaction of different systems lies at the root of Bill Liao's venture, WeForest. As an entrepreneur and social networking pioneer, Bill has been exposed to a broad range of industries, thinkers and practitioners from across the world. As a neo-generalist he has sought to connect skills and capabilities from different sectors, adopting a holistic, big-picture perspective, to address one of the pressing climate change issues: global warming. For Bill it has been a case of gaining an education in environmental matters, then seeking ways to teach others about them and put new ideas into action, whether through the work of WeForest or in his book *Forests*. Boiled down to its essence, the idea behind WeForest is a simple one. It benefits from the synthesis of expertise and scientific knowledge; the compilation of a metanarrative that has entailed the uncovering of clues in one discipline and their exposure to another. Cloud cover, created by the release of water vapour, not only serves as a source of fresh water for our lakes and rivers but also has the added advantage of reflecting solar radiation back into space. Such cloud cover can be generated by trees, which also absorb excess CO_2 from the atmosphere. It follows, therefore, that a reforestation programme could provide a natural means of tackling, or at least slowing, the effects of global warming. WeForest aims to plant two trillion trees by 2020. In addition, WeForest is seeking to restore soil quality, supporting the growth of trees and food crops, and reversing the effects of overgrazing and desertification.

Maggie MacDonald is another environmental campaigner who lives in multiple worlds, spanning activism, leadership development and the arts. While she acknowledges the chimeric aspect of her plural life, Maggie makes a conscious choice to compartmentalise the different things she does. Nevertheless, as with Briony, there are inevitable synergies between her various activities, pattern matches and overlaps. Maggie's experiences as writer and performer provide another lens through which to assess and distil her interests in change leadership, community and environmental issues. Her role as an activist, connecting NGO to community to government agencies, typifies that of the neo-generalist. Like Ai Weiwei in China, she can switch from artistic creativity to raising social awareness about big issues, often blending the two. She crosses domain boundaries, brokering knowledge, effecting change. The power of story is essential to her interaction with these different groups as she seeks to influence policy that impacts on public health and environmental concerns.

It is an experience shared by Ella Saltmarshe. She too transcends the worlds of non-profit campaigning and the creative arts, where she writes short stories, children's fiction and screenplays for feature films and soap opera television. Ella advises NGOs, donors and governments on strategic philanthropy, public policy and social change. She has an academic background in anthropology, which adds another dimension to her understanding of story and how it can engage people in fundamental ways. She has applied these skills to non-profit case studies written to influence key decision-makers among civil servants. For Ella, story is a means of packaging human experience into narrative, of helping us understand the world and our lives. Her own restless curiosity and neo-generalism provides an endless source of new knowledge and story material.

Certain trends begin to emerge: the wandering and curiosity of the flâneur, the pattern recognition and sense-making capabilities of the detective, the storytelling and communication abilities of the writer and artist, are all useful approaches to adopt as we gain awareness of an ever-shifting, volatile world. The entrepreneurial Ting Kelly's master–apprentice relationship with her father, Kevin Kelly, and her learning journey adventures in Asia with her partner, Bjorn Cooley, illustrate how powerful the endless search for knowledge can be, how it equips the inquisitive with new skills. People are looking to others to guide them even as they themselves learn how to navigate the complexities of a networked world. The edges between virtual and physical, online and offline, inside and outside, are blurring. Bridge builders are required. Mapmakers too. Explorers who will simplify and translate what they discover, laying out suggested paths for others to follow. Tricksters who will step over boundaries and confuse neat black-and-white categorisations, exposing the continuums that lie in-between.

Throughout the history of humankind, our explorers, scientists, inventors and artists have constantly reshaped the boundaries between the known and the unknown. Whether at sea, jungle-bound, in a laboratory, before a canvas or with the first tentative steps on the moon they have erased old edges and drawn in new ones – for others to smudge and redefine in the future. Their endeavours help simplify the chaotic for the rest of us. They overlay new patterns that they have recognised, erect signposts and markers to guide us, beacons to light our way. They enact the cycle of knowledge mastery, seeking, sensing and sharing as they go. Of course, their maps are ultimately personal. They reflect their own cultural context, ideology, preferences and prejudices. The map is an opportunity to impose their own vision, to channel their own beliefs and values and thereby influence others. Mental landscapes become entwined and intermingled with physical ones. Reality and fiction merge, if they were ever distinct in the first place. Writing itself becomes a form of mapmaking. So too our digital journeys via the hyperlink.

Peter Morville argues in *Intertwingled* that the way we organise, shape, categorise and architect information is another form of cartography, of storytelling, another process for knowledge mastery. But the maps themselves are constantly transforming. We have to keep retuning, exercising our sense-making skills not only to guide others but ourselves as well. For, at the edge of our maps, everything remains hazy, slipping in and out of focus. Everything is liminal, caught between two states, containing yet more revelations just beyond the threshold of our understanding. The neo-generalist continues to scan for patterns and attempts to interpret what they see. In such circumstances, to borrow from Baudelaire's *The Painter of Modern Life*, they can be likened 'to a kaleidoscope endowed with consciousness, which with every one of its movements presents a pattern of life, in all its multiplicity, and the flowing grace of all the elements that go to compose life'.

Some, like change agent and artist Peter Vander Auwera, turn their lives into a quest for understanding. The process of detection provides a sense of purpose. Patterns are recognised, one clue is linked to another, choices are made. In Peter's case, this requires him to assume leadership responsibilities, acting as facilitator, serving as an impresario, a ring master, who brings others together in communities, at events, to share their insights and collectively translate their learning into action. Anne McCrossan, on the other hand, speaks of her experience living in other countries, the feeling of culture shock, of having no compass with which to navigate the unfamiliar. The focus shifts to creating new maps, new forms of navigation. It requires planning for the future while respecting what has been learned in the past; encouraging others to find comfort in ambiguity, excitement in the unknown – like Brother William guiding the novice Adso as they venture into the labyrinthine library guarded by Jorge of Burgos. It is to the neo-generalist as leader and playmaker that we now turn our attention.

NO. 10

True leaders are stewards of the future.
They take responsibility for
adding to the legacy.

James Kerr, Legacy

It is early evening on Saturday 31 October 2015. Sonny Bill Williams receives the ball in open play, draws in three defenders and offloads in characteristic style to Ben Smith on the wing. Smith kicks the ball into touch and the match is brought to a close, having boiled to a thrilling climax. Moments before, the All Blacks fly-half, Dan Carter, had converted Beauden Barrett's late try to earn the final points of the match in New Zealand's 34-17 victory over Australia. It has been one of the most entertaining finals in the short history of the Rugby World Cup. Compelling, emotional, masterful in its execution. Even as the ball is passed to Williams, there is a tannoy announcement in the stadium identifying Carter as the man of the match. A fairy-tale ending for an illustrious international career. But for so long it was doubtful whether Carter would be here at all.

This is a story of several such talented individuals cohering as a team. One of immense talent, culture, community and application in the face of adversity. Carter is among the most lauded rugby union players in the professional era of the sport. He is recognised by many as the finest fly-half ever to have played the game, elevating his all-round craft to a level not previously witnessed. He has been named the International Rugby Board's player of the year on three separate occasions, holds the world record for the most points scored in test match rugby, and has experienced success as a member of All Black squads that have regularly won the Tri Nations and Rugby Championship competitions, defeated the British and Irish Lions and won back-to-back World Cup tournaments in 2011 and 2015. Of the 112 matches Carter played for the All Blacks, he experienced victory in 99 matches and drew only once.

His personal success as the final whistle is blown is not greeted with complacency. No one is bigger than the team, and he is but one part of the collective. Instead, relief and humility characterise these final moments on the biggest stage. It is a salve for lingering pain. During the 2011 World Cup hosted in his own country, the talismanic fly-half's involvement was curtailed by injury. He was a non-playing squad member when his teammates lifted the trophy, his communal delight mixed with personal frustration. Further injury problems followed during an international sabbatical playing domestic rugby in France. As the 2015 tournament approached, injury and form raised questions about his participation. His master-class performance in the final, then, not only bids adieu to the international stage but puts several ghosts to rest. His winner's medal has been earned by right this time around rather than by association.

Carter's personal history on the rugby field, like that of teammate and captain Richie McCaw, is closely aligned with the trials, tribulations and transformation of the national team during the current century up to that unprecedented World Cup double. New Zealand is a proud rugby-playing nation with an unparalleled history of success in the sport. It has become entwined with the nation's cultural heritage in the same way that football has in Brazil. When New Zealand won the first Rugby World Cup in 1987, there was an expectation that this would be repeated over and over again. Between the four-year tournament cycles, the All Blacks did indeed dominate the world stage, entering each competition as one of the favourites but never quite achieving their goal until a nail-biting 8-7 victory over France in the 2011 final.

The turning point in the All Blacks' fortunes came at the 2007 tournament when the same team, France, defeated them at the quarter-final stage. This failure had a catalytic effect, prompting a reassessment of culture, purpose and values within the All Blacks set-up, involving administrators, coaching staff and players. The impact of this is documented in James Kerr's book-length study *Legacy*. It is also central to the stories and analogies that sports scientist and leadership consultant Al Smith shared with us during our numerous discussions about neo-generalism with him. Al highlights how the lessons learned from the All Blacks' transformation, and the importance of culture to this, has relevance far beyond the sporting domain. They can be applied in a political context, in corporations, in any organisational structure. Indeed, the All Blacks themselves have been open to the influence of other coaching methods and ideas, sourced from other sports but also from the realms of business, philosophy and psychology as well.

It is evident from the way that the All Blacks operate today that everyone is in this together, that everyone has a voice, regardless of hierarchical seniority, age, position or job title. Everyone is a leader, everyone serves others with humility and respect, prioritising the collective *we* over the glory of the individual *me*. No matter who you are, there will be times when it will be you sweeping out the changing rooms after a training session. Anyone wearing an All Blacks jersey wants to be the best they can possibly be. This requires continuous learning, improvement and adaptation. Changing your own game, when it seems you have reached the pinnacle. Helping your opponents advance, sharing coaching tips, so you too can develop your game further in order to be better than them. Only when you are at your best, the theory goes, can I reach my best too.

At the core of the All Blacks mentality is the notion of legacy. Honouring what has gone before but also preparing the way for what is to follow. It is the idea of being a good ancestor. Once an All Black, always an All Black. Even as New Zealand celebrated their 2015 World Cup victory, for example, this notion of legacy was powerfully reflected as the nation mourned the death of one of its great international stars, Jonah Lomu. The haka performed by the national team before the start of each match, by mourners at Lomu's memorial service and by former teammates at the French roadside location where Jerry Collins died in a car accident root this in Māori culture. It respects the diversity of the New Zealand populace. It connects the team to the country. This is why someone like Sonny Boy Williams feels able to give his World Cup winner's medal away, only moments after receiving it, to a 14-year-old fan when he sees him being harshly treated by security personnel.

Legacy is there from the beginning. So too a sense of belonging. Every time someone becomes an All Black they are given a small, leather-bound book. The first pages include images of jerseys that reflect the history and success of the New Zealand team from 1905 to the present. The remaining pages are blank, waiting to be filled with the individual's personal story, their legacy. The challenge that each new team member confronts is to leave their jersey in a better place than they found it, to add a specific legacy to the idea of being an All Black, to the position they play and to the number that denotes that position.

In Dan Carter's case, that is the number 10. This is the pivotal position of fly-half. Like the quarterback in American football or the number 10 in football, this is a playmaker role, a distributor and guide. The 10 is the organiser of defence and initiator of attack; a leader who reassures and inspires their teammates, creating time and space in which they can flourish. Announcing his first squad as the new England coach in January 2016, Eddie Jones observed, 'The 10 has got to be the bus driver and the servant. He has to know which route to take and know what the team needs to have.' The 10 is the puppeteer. The fly-half manoeuvres and kicks for field position. They accumulate points with hand and boot. All in service of the team's objectives rather than in pursuit of personal glory. In Carter's case, the record books stand testament to his fulfilment of the role, his acceptance of these varied responsibilities. Like England's Jonny Wilkinson before him, Carter could be metronomic in his goal kicking, constantly keeping the scoreboard moving. But he could also be electric in attack. He scanned for gaps and opportunities, playing what was in front of him, having the confidence to act on his own initiative rather than feeling constrained by a preconceived game plan. The performances of those who stood alongside him were also raised to another level. Through personal excellence, he brought out the best in others.

The same can be observed of the great number 10s in football. Pelé, Puskás, Maradona, Laudrup, Zidane and Messi possessed mesmeric skill and goal-scoring capability. But they also demonstrated exceptional leadership qualities, able to inspire teammates on the pitch and fans in the stadiums, bars and living rooms with their actions, their intuition and responsiveness. As masters of imagination and peripheral vision, they specialised in the unpredictable pass that ripped the opponents' defence apart and settled games. Dennis Bergkamp, another 10, reflects on this in his autobiography, *Stillness and Speed*, when he comments on the need to adapt to context, to draw on knowledge and experience so that, unconsciously, the situation creates the move. As playmaker, the 10 is always inventing, creating in the moment, alert and sensitive to opportunity. For this to be effective, however, they require strong trust-based relationships with those around them. Where they lead, others have to be willing to follow.

This emphasis on leadership, on the development of leadership capability throughout a team, is not unique to sport. However, it is from the fields and waters of sporting endeavour that many lessons are learned and translated for application in other arenas. Al Smith brings a particularly neo-generalist approach to this, whether working in the health sector and academia, or with British Rowing and UK Sport, or as an independent consultant. Al switches in and out of specialisms, blending clinical experience as a physiologist with quantitative sports science and more qualitative coaching expertise. In an archetypal neo-generalist trajectory,

Al has taken a nomadic approach to his career. Frequently, he has found himself an interloper, a trickster from another domain, who borrows knowledge and ideas from one field in order to cross-pollinate them with those from another. He is a learning dynamicist, acquiring new skills and experience even as he coaches and mentors others, blending thought leadership with practical application. This is as relevant to helping an individual be the best they can be through sport as it is to team performance or the delivery of community projects.

An appreciation of complex, adaptive systems is central to Al's work. How do leaders develop the skills to navigate complexity? How do teams, whether of the sporting, corporate or non-profit variety, become adaptive so that they can respond effectively to contextual shifts? How do trust-dependent communities enable leadership and knowledge to flow to the right places at the right time? How does a balanced system allow for autonomy, creativity and intuition while still serving a collective purpose? Al's intertwingled approach has led him to explore how individual and collective performance is not uniquely presented through numbers and data analysis. In the sporting domain, it requires an understanding of the physical, the physiological and the psychological too. In any domain, it also necessitates an appreciation of context and environment. It is through this holistic, integrated perspective that incremental gains are identified and attained.

A common mantra, often heard in interviews with athletes, coaches and sports directors, is that focus should be on process rather than desired goal. Get the process right, they say, and the results will follow. This is not process in the constraining sense that we associate with the business world, preserved in the aspic of rulebooks, mired in bureaucracy, measured repetitively and often meaninglessly. It is process as a more adaptive, collaborative endeavour. Process humanised. It is something that rarely stands still but is subject to continuous refinement and evolution.

It is shaped by both human input and human action. The same process-as-pattern that Briony Marshall talks of in relation to artistic creation, or that Ed Catmull references in *Creativity, Inc.* in relation to the fusion of people, art and computer science that underpins the development of an animated Pixar movie. The identification, frequent adjustment and consistent improvement of good practice.

There is an important distinction to draw out here between the notion of *good* and *best* practice. *Best* practice belongs to the mindset of the hedgehog. There is a single right way of doing something. A summit has been attained, a flag planted. This is the method that will be imposed, enforced if necessary, on all others. There are clearly delineated steps, tasks and roles. The problem here is that gradual progression is denied. The moment we lock something down like this is the moment entropy sets in. The only way things can be transformed will be suddenly and radically, at the edges, in keeping with the pattern of punctuated equilibrium. *Good* practice, on the other hand, belongs to the fox. It is adaptive, responding to progressive steps, marginal gains. It evolves with the ecosystem rather than trying to constrain it. It is owned collectively. There is room for invention, for personal expression. Such insight can benefit the neo-generalist leader, even in the most complex of situations.

John Michel tells an anecdote from his experiences serving as a general with the US Air Force in Afghanistan. John arrived in 2013, several years into a stop-start initiative to re-establish an Afghan Air Force led by the NATO Air Training Command–Afghanistan. Four factors drew his attention: An accelerated deadline was now in place as President Obama had brought forward the date for withdrawal of US military personnel from Afghanistan. The current Air Force initiative was not sustainable as it would be too expensive given other demands on the post-conflict Afghan national budget. Aircraft maintenance, one of the most essential requirements for the effective running of an air force, was being carried out by NATO crews with no local involvement. There was too great a reliance throughout the programme on NATO specialists and third-party consultants.

John brought these foreign experts and Afghan representatives together. The experts outlined what was required going forwards. When John asked the locals what they thought, he was astonished to discover that this was the first time their opinion had been sought since the inception of the programme. The imposition of best practice now gave way to the co-creation of good practice and the identification of an effective solution. The role of leader and follower ebbed and flowed, shaped by context. Local knowledge of terrain and community was blended with NATO knowledge of aviation and combat. John was able to facilitate this networked expertise, using his hierarchical position to nurture and steward rather than to command and control.

As a fighter pilot, John started his military career as a well-educated and highly-trained specialist. What he discovered with the passage of time, however, was that his association with the US Air Force afforded him the opportunity to diversify and generalise in a number of ways. The son of French immigrants to the United States, whose father had himself served in the US military, John spent some of his childhood in both France and Germany. He subsequently served in Europe, as well as in conflict zones such as Iraq and Afghanistan. The experiences taught him to develop an understanding of different cultures and people, to empathise and use emotional intelligence, skills which he learned to apply in leadership roles both at home and overseas.

Before retiring from active service and moving into consultancy, John had experienced fourteen roles with the US Air Force, all of them somewhat different from those he had performed previously. As a result, he became increasingly aware that the more successful you are in the military, the more generalist you become. This is reflected by the rank of Brigadier General that he ultimately attained. It was far removed from the specialism of the fighter pilot. The generalist general is someone who transcends specialism and applies themselves across multiple fields. They connect the specialists, helping them understand how they fit in and contribute to the big picture. John, who during his military service also acquired a PhD in transformational leadership, understood that his role was to think, manoeuvre, create conditions for success, lead change, facilitate and communicate in a variety of different contexts.

John's engagement of Afghan nationals and co-creation of a strategic plan for a new Afghan Air Force was a natural application of these responsibilities. It required the development of a story that spanned from the historic past through the present partnership of NATO forces and Afghan military to a future of cost-effective Afghan self-sufficiency and security. As with the All Blacks, it was underpinned by the notion of legacy, something with both roots and a future. Neo-generalist leadership, true stewardship, bridges through both time and space. There is a responsibility to tradition and ancestry, a duty of care to those in the here and now, and a requirement to serve those who will come. There is an element of synthesis, pulling together many different elements to paint a picture of the future, of listening and learning, of guidance and teaching, of both confidence and humility, of playmaking at scale rather than on a single field of endeavour. The ultimate goal of the transformational leader is to make yourself redundant.

To continue the rugby analogy, imagine you are standing in a backline. You receive the ball from a figure in the past, delicately floated for you to run on to and catch without breaking your stride. You in turn pass the ball at the correct height for someone in the future to gather. The legacy is a never-ending backline, with the ball always in motion, passed from one set of hands to another, joining past and future in the present. It captures Ed Catmull's aspiration that the Pixar culture so carefully nurtured by himself, Steve Jobs and John Lasseter outlasts the founders and evolves into the future. As well as Jiro Ono's desire for his sons to progress from long-term apprenticeship to mastery so that they continue the family tradition of serving the highest quality sushi. On a grander scale, it reflects the work Erika Ilves and her colleagues are doing, seeking out alternative planetary environments to support human life and the future of our species. As well as the numerous projects conducted by the Long Now Foundation, which operates on a 10,000-year clock.

FUTURE

PRESENT

PAST

*[**Figure 10.1.** Passing through time]*

This is what Charles Handy, in *The Empty Raincoat*, calls cathedral philosophy. The idea draws as much on lessons from the natural world as it does from humankind's interaction with and shaping of their landscape. It provides a metaphor for transformational leadership that extends beyond one's own time. Consider the example of La Grotte des Demoiselles, which can be found near Saint Bauzille de Putois in the Languedoc region of France. This has been crafted over an expanse of millions of years as water has eroded and hollowed out sections of limestone. The Grotte is a living museum of enormous stalactites and stalagmites that have developed at a steady, incremental rate through the millennia. The result, especially in the central cavern known as the Cathédrale des Abîmes, is breathtaking. The Cathédrale is filled with columns and pillars, as well as structures that look like stone forests and shoals of jellyfish. There is even a stalagmite towards the bottom of the Cathédrale that could be a man-made statue of the Virgin and Child. The chamber is a natural wonder, so magnificent and surreal in structure and artistry, that it seems not of this world. It resembles a set lifted from cinematic fantasy, straight from the mind of a film magician like George Méliès.

Many of the structures contained in the cavernous depths of the Grotte are unwittingly replicated in medieval places of worship, as well as the Gothic reworkings of later centuries. These echo and mirror the ornamentation and natural artistry of the Cathédrale. Both have required an investment of time to take on their current form. In the case of Chartres Cathedral, for example, the current edifice was completed in 1250 after a construction period of 56 years. This was during an era when life expectancy was significantly shorter than it is today, which means many builders and artisans contributed to the construction and ornamentation of the cathedral for the benefit of those that followed them, never seeing the completed building themselves. In subsequent generations, medieval cathedrals would be repurposed as temples of reason by members of the Enlightenment.

New, secular forms of cathedral would follow too, in the form of the factories, railway terminals, bridges and power stations of the Industrial Revolution. These too would undergo transformation and remodelling as human needs shifted.

With the rise of the knowledge worker, the former monuments to carbon-fuelled manual industries themselves metamorphosed into galleries, restaurants, dwellings and hubs for start-up enterprises. At the same time, digital temples of reason were created, inhabited by people who commune in both virtual and physical spaces. These are communities and movements that have been built through the hyperlink; the connection of people and knowledge facilitated by fluctuating networks. Our new cathedrals are digital spaces and human communities. Such international networks do not recognise the constraints of time and space. The neo-generalist leader has to be a playmaker across other dimensions, not just the physical world. They are the pupils of Grace Clapham and Solonia Teodros's Change School: adept network navigators, change catalysts and global citizens. In one dimension, they pass the ball with the speed of a mouse click, creating opportunities for people dispersed around the world to make the next move. In another, there is the slow progression, the long-term view, constantly adapting to change, the merger, atomisation, transformation and decline of organisations.

As Charles phrases it in his autobiography, 'Death is a useful deadline, a reminder that life is our brief opportunity to create something that might outlast us.' It is a topic that fascinates Geoffrey West, a theoretical physicist and former president of the Santa Fe Institute who encourages and practises a transdisciplinary approach to addressing life's big questions, attempting to discover the rules that underpin everything. In his case, this means combining mathematics, physics, biology, business and economics in order to develop an understanding of complex systems like cities and corporations. What emerges is an appreciation of both longevity and legacy. As with biological life forms, from plants to bears to humans, cities and organisations tend to have finite lifespans. In order to survive and flourish, there is a need to change and adapt before the current evolutionary path plateaus, ossifies and an inevitable decline sets in. It is the crucial moment when the playmaker makes their pass.

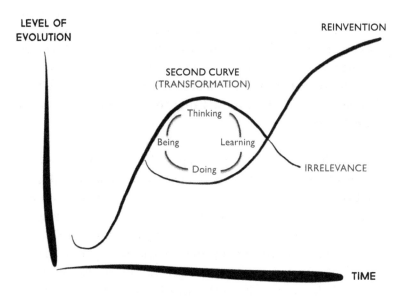

*[**Figure 10.2.** The second curve]*

This is a phenomenon that Geoffrey and Charles have discovered independently of one another, what the latter refers to as *The Second Curve*. Both use the metaphor of a sigmoid curve to describe the arc that an individual, an organisation, a system undertakes. It is before the upper slopes of the elongated S are reached that a new sigmoid curve needs to begin – the ball to be passed – to ensure both transition and legacy. If this does not happen, it becomes increasingly difficult to change, energy is lost from the system and there is an acceleration into an entropic decline and demise. John Gardner argues in *Self-Renewal* that it is as organisations lose their vitality that specialisation becomes entrenched. The inevitable silo perspectives that we associate with the compartmentalisation of functional capabilities follow. Flexibility and fluidity are lost. Failure of different organs results in final collapse.

History offers an interesting example. The leadership of change requires knowing when to pass the ball, an understanding of context and empathy for those who will be affected by the transition. In the wake of World War I, these ingredients were missing as the victorious allies sought to break up the Ottoman Empire. Actions were determined by the myopia of expertise rather than the big-picture vision of neo-generalism. In 1921 Winston Churchill, in his capacity as the British Colonial Secretary, was required to oversee the Cairo Conference. Economist John Maynard Keynes warned that interference in the Middle East would foment a volatility that would still be evident in the region a hundred years into the future. His admonitions fell on deaf ears. It is this kind of shoddy legacy that John Michel and others are trying to unpick today in countries like Iraq and Syria. Legacy is not always beneficial. As Robin Chase points out, the term *legacy system* rarely has positive connotations. It is more suggestive of constraint than evolutionary progression or the foundation for creative innovation.

Via the office of the British Prime Minister and their official London residence, 10 Downing Street, the number 10 has become synonymous with political leadership too. This requires play-making on a grander stage, with the composition of teams – from cabinets, to coalitions, to military and economic alliances – in a constant state of flux. There is an ever-present tension for such elected officials between the cult of personality that helped them secure office, convincing the electorate that they were worth backing, and the requirement to service the needs of that same electorate and the future generations that will follow them. For some, however, the lure of personal legacy and historical status outweighs the responsibility to steward for the future. Economic uncertainty, military conflicts, mass migration and environmental disaster tend to be treated from a siloed, just-in-time perspective rather than holistically and for the long term. As a consequence, governments change often, either through reshuffles or elections, as prone to the sigmoid curve as any other organism.

Too often politicians present themselves as the fixers of mistakes made by the previous incumbents. Their eyes are fixed on the rear-view mirror rather than looking to the future through the windscreen. There are some nations that remain hamstrung by their imperialist past or their aspirations to establish a modern empire. They have inherited the mindset of the hedgehog, of antecedents who sought to impose their ways not only at home but on subject nations too. The break-up of former empires, the emergence of new superpowers, adds to the global volatility. Subject nations throw off the constraints of past regimes, but enter a period of youthful experimentation, until they get their own backlines moving fluidly again, the ball passing seamlessly through the ages.

The variety of political systems adds intrigue to the mix. In some countries there is a deliberate separation of powers, which means that people responsible for important state functions like education, health, the economy, foreign affairs and defence cannot be elected officials. This happens in republics, where presidents nominate their preferred candidates for approval by the national legislature. What tends to happen, therefore, is that individuals with deep expertise in narrow fields are appointed to these key positions. The whole system is founded on the notion of compartmentalisation. In other nations, ministers can only be appointed from the pool of elected officials. Cabinet members are required to fulfil a designated portfolio and simultaneously serve their constituents. In the latter system there is frequent movement from one portfolio to another. The ministers are generalists who rely on the expertise of the civil servants they work with. The one constant in either system, until the next election or scandal, tends to be the president or prime minister. They are always adapting to context, moving across the neo-generalist continuum, regardless of their former profession or specialist domain.

The October 2015 election in Canada begins a story that will be fascinating to follow over the coming years. Victory was secured by the Liberal Party and, in an interesting twist on the notion of legacy, allowed Justin Trudeau to follow in his father's footsteps as the nation's Prime Minister. Trudeau's first cabinet challenged the status quo in Western countries, in which political leadership is all too often dominated by ageing white males. In seeking to confront issues that affect today's society and be prepared to take advantage of opportunities for tomorrow's, Trudeau chose to bring together an ethnically diverse, youthful, gender-balanced team, expressing a desire to work with a cabinet that represented the multicultural nation in microcosm. By blending a range of perspectives and experience, Trudeau appears to evidence the enlightened self-interest that Prasad Kaipa and Navi Radjou argue is essential to wise leadership. He has shifted emphasis on to collective service and action that will benefit national legacy. Already he is thinking about leaving the jersey in a better place.

Robin Chase builds a compelling case for this in *Peers Inc*. Motivated by the big issues of climate change, population growth and migration, Robin is urging governments, corporations, NGOs and independents to come together to design and enact solutions. She draws on her experience as the co-founder of Zipcar, her involvement in other platform-based ventures, and her deep understanding of the power of networked knowledge and fluid leadership. In order to establish a legacy for future generations, there is an urgent need to shift the trajectory of the current narrative, which points to significant rises in temperatures, carbon pollution and sea levels. By 2100, as many as half the current species on the planet could face extinction, the number of people living in cities is likely to have reached unprecedented levels, the incidence of resource-related conflicts could have escalated even further, prompting ever great movement of people away from zones affected by war and environmental collapse. It is a bleak picture.

A good leader is a good teacher. They educate others, developing the next generation of leaders. Robin uses her writing, her public speaking and board level involvement to inform and enlighten. She seeks to influence other leaders across diverse domains, from politics to business to academia, encouraging them to help change the narrative and improve the legacy. Robin earned a joint honours degree in English, French and Philosophy, then studied business administration and design as a postgraduate. The daughter of a diplomat, her childhood education spanned seven countries and thirteen schools. She is used to traversing and impacting many worlds. As an entrepreneur, Robin advocates the sharing of resources, allowing for more efficient use of them. She promotes the collaborative interaction of organisations and individuals, with the former opening their platforms and the latter leveraging what they can from them through innovation, localisation and customisation.

Her ideas have had a significant impact on the transportation sector. With Zipcar, the focus was on making use of excess capacity: cars standing idle in the street or parking lot for most of the day. Robin and her colleagues implemented a technologically-enabled infrastructure based on vehicles, IT systems and smartphone apps. Customers book cars for the time they need them. They limit their personal expenditure on driving (car ownership, insurance, parking fees), minimise the number of car journeys they make, and help reduce carbon pollution as a consequence. A similar model has been adopted in ride-share initiatives and different forms of taxi service. Robin highlights how a form of carbon taxation at the platform level, not only in the transport industry but across all sectors, could add further to the environmental legacy of these emerging business models.

Concerns with value creation rather than value extraction are also present in Anand Mahindra's leadership. In contemporary markets a short-term fixation on maximising shareholder value is widespread. But to create lasting value, fulfilling a higher purpose is key for humans and organisations alike. Anand advocates that successful businesses in the twenty-first century will be those who create value for a wider community and align their interests for mutual benefit and well-being. Any company can claim that they exist to drive positive change in society but delivering on such a grand promise is difficult.

For the Mahindra Group this is much more than simply a marketing or corporate social responsibility (CSR) activity that can be appended to existing practice. The company's stated purpose is to help people rise, to enable transformation and positive change. Financial success is viewed as an outcome of doing good in the world. Anand is a custodian of values, a caretaker of continuity and progress. Custodians hold something in trust on behalf of others. It is a dual role of seeing gaps between what is and what could be. Inherently, it goes beyond finding answers to what and how things are done. It also implies making moral choices and value judgements in a volatile and ever-shifting environment. Foresight and responsiveness are prerequisites for transformation and mastery of the second curve.

Leadership is enacted every day, by all of us, regardless of titles and formal responsibilities. Neo-generalist leaders are comfortable with the ambiguity of white noise. By wandering a rugged path, they have learned how to learn. The search for an identity beyond the confinement of labels makes them natural shapeshifters. They master the art of building bridges between people and ideas, seeing the whole picture rather than just a fragment of it. Natural curiosity leads them to change their perspective, expanding their peripheral view as required. They recognise patterns and know how to make sense of subtle clues. Constantly they examine and critique how they think, learn, act and live. It is such habits that shape their legacy.

PART

III

II.
SHADOWS

They are the elemental particles making up the work's nucleus, around which all the rest revolves. Or else like the void at the bottom of a vortex which sucks in and swallows currents.

Italo Calvino, *If on a Winter's Night a Traveller*

Despite their cultural diversity and their multidimensional professional backgrounds, one thing unites the interviewees for this book. That is their high level of literacy, their consumption of the written word in analogue and digital format. They are readers of books, frequently multiple books simultaneously, of blog posts, newspaper articles and academic papers. A common port of call is *Brain Pickings*, an online service curated by Maria Popova. The draw is the quality of the writing, as well as the creative combination of art, science, business, design, psychology, fiction, poetry, children's literature and philosophy. The site comes with a health warning: any visit can result in a debit in the bank account, as people progress from Popova's inspirational posts and on to book stores in order to purchase the numerous new recommendations they have encountered.

One of the many anecdotes Popova relates concerns Picasso. The great artist is spotted on a park bench by a fan, eventually submitting to a request to sketch her portrait. Within minutes he hands over the drawing, prompting an enthusiastic response from its subject. When she enquires how much she owes him, she is shocked to hear him quote a figure of $5,000. How is that possible, she wants to know, for only five minutes of endeavour? To which Picasso responds, 'No, madam, it took me my whole life.' Mark Storm, a transformation design consultant, tells a similar anecdote regarding an occasion when he provided an insightful observation that helped colleagues significantly change the focus of the bid they were working on. When they secured a contract with the new client, he was informed that he could bill a couple of hours to the project. He experienced physical recoil at the suggestion and a fundamental sense of being misunderstood.

This gets to the nub of one of the issues that confronts the neo-generalist. Their experience cannot be measured, and they forever face the struggle of making the value of what they do visible. As innovation process expert Sarah Miller Caldicott frames it, borrowing from the dehumanising language of the quantifiers, 'How do you determine the return on investment of a generalist?' The observation Mark made to his colleagues rested on deep and broad foundations. It did not just derive from professional expertise, but from a potent mix of the extracurricular books he had read, the conversations he had had, the networks he had navigated and contributed to, his appreciation of art and philosophy, the insights he had gained from travelling. His ability to blend and cross-pollinate from this wealth of accumulated knowledge and lived experience enabled him to make the observation that he did. What for colleagues was a momentary contribution, for Mark was a case of drawing on a life's learning, a life's work. In a world still keeping step to the tune of managerial measurement practices, how does the neo-generalist stay true to their values while gaining recognition for what they do?

Our conversations with Mark and several other interviewees illustrate that there is a darker side to neo-generalism, one shaped by lack of understanding and appreciation. James Tyer also suggests that the breadth of interests of a neo-generalist means that they always have more ideas than they can ever act upon, more books and articles lined up than they can ever read. That can be personally overwhelming. Conversely, however, the neo-generalist's creative mix of these ideas can be too much for those around them; the vision they paint too futuristic for mindsets stuck in the past. For some, this is hugely problematic, genuinely inhibiting. Resistance is wearing and, without good self-management, can quickly lead to burnout. For others, they fall back on contrarian, non-conformist behaviour. When undervalued in the workplace, several have sought out external communities through which they can exercise their social activism and change agency. But, given their feistiness, they are quick to leave them if they find that rules and regulations curtail the autonomy within loose frameworks they aspire to. Personal idealism is often found to be in tension with the reality of working effectively with partners motivated by slightly different agendas.

Simon Heath is an entertaining and insightful visual communicator. He neatly captures this contrarianism when he describes himself as an expert generalist and cynical optimist. Even in writing this book, we have found that at times we have been specialists on generalism, at others generalists on specialism. It is all part and parcel of those fluctuating and disjointed travels on the neo-generalist continuum. There is, however, an element of existential angst to all of this. To make ourselves understood, even in a playful, self-derogatory way, we have had to adopt other people's labels, position ourselves, however temporarily, in other people's pigeonholes. Only the very successful, like Charles Handy, manage to sidestep the issue by turning themselves into a brand, their business cards stripped of all labels but their own name. Many of our interviewees, though, suggest that this urge to categorise has its most insidious effects in the workplace, as relevant to the start-up entrepreneur seeking funding as to the corporate employee trapped within a rigid hierarchy.

It is worth returning to one of our personal stories to illuminate this. Richard started his career as a freelance writer and editor before becoming an employee at a variety of private, public and non-profit organisations. After fifteen years, he chose to accept the offer of voluntary redundancy and become self-employed again. He opted to focus anew on writing and editing, dependent now on accumulated knowledge and practical skills, as well as a more clearly defined purpose. As a writer he could give expression to his polymathic generalism. As a book doctor and mentor to other writers, he could draw not only on his editorial experience but his varied subject matter expertise too. The change would mean no longer having to commute for four hours a day, more time with his family and a greater sense of personal well-being. The big question mark, though, centred on whether such a venture was economically viable.

Therein lies another paradox. The freedom and portfolio life of the independent lends itself well to neo-generalism. It is a realm of ambiguity, constant learning, trial and error. Family life, though, demands a degree of financial stability and security, underpinned by the parents' commitment to and responsibility for their children. It is characterised by the known and the routine. This sort of security is often derived via employment, the kind of job under our current system of education, recruitment and career progression where you have to demonstrate a deep specialism even to get through the door for an interview; where generalist tendencies still can be perceived as a shortcoming rather than a strength. The question is, do you succumb and hide once again behind the categorisation and labels of others to help them understand at least part of who you are and what you do? Is it possible to ever really belong in such a situation?

Even as this book was being developed and written, Richard opted to explore the job market, seeking out new opportunities, constantly bumping up against the specialist mindset. It was an experience both demoralising and gratifying. Gratifying in that it reinforced his conviction that there is a systemic failure that needs highlighting through books like this and the communities that advocate new ways of thinking, organising and working. Demoralising because he was constantly being forced to look backwards rather than forwards. This came from dealing with recruitment agencies and the algorithms of online services like LinkedIn. There is an emphasis in such interactions on what you have done rather than on possibility, on what you could do in the future. Your own words, on a curriculum vitae or a social profile, are used to define the cookie cutter. Boundary crossing is frowned upon. Only the most recent experience or role really matters. No thought will be given to how you might combine your diversity of experience into a unique offering.

The contrarian wants to challenge the job descriptions, to offer a different way of thinking about roles, responsibilities, leadership and change, to deflect the constraint of a job title. The financially-constrained parent pushes on with the application. The rejection letters pile up. *Too experienced. We think you would be bored. Missing a piece of the jigsaw puzzle. The label does not fit. We do not know how to categorise you. Too public sector. You are not one of us. You confuse us. You scare us.* How does the neo-generalist persuade the potential employer that it is through the very multi-dimensionality of their experience that they will add value to the organisation? That through their inherent curiosity and desire to learn they will quickly plug gaps in knowledge? That as a bridge to other communities and disciplines they will expose the organisation to different ways of thinking and doing? That their outsider status can have a catalytic effect on innovation and creativity?

Change agent and business adviser Simon Terry describes a seminal experience while an employee at a retail bank in Australia. For Simon, his strength is his neo-generalism, his ability to synthesise ideas from diverse academic, personal research and workplace experiences in law, analysis, business development, sales, marketing and financial services. He then shapes them into actionable knowledge, influencing innovation and transformation. Simon can scan broadly and apply narrowly. This he did to great effect at the bank, only to be informed by the CEO that his generalism was perceived as a problem. It rendered him difficult to categorise, which meant that whenever promotion opportunities arose, he would always be overlooked. Only through the visible demonstration of deep expertise in a specialist field can recognition be gained in situations like these. The ability to add value across numerous fields may be acknowledged but rarely rewarded. It points to a disparity in the earning potential between specialists and generalists in traditional organisational structures.

Sadly, Simon's story is far from uncommon. A study of type-casting in Hollywood conducted by Ezra Zuckerman of the MIT Sloan School of Management sheds more light on the matter. Here too specialism is institutionalised, which means that generalists, when compared with those who are content to limit their range, are always at risk of earning less and failing to secure roles over the span of their acting lives. It is not the chameleons but the one-trick ponies who enjoy the more lucrative careers on the silver screen. Zuckerman finds that similar typecasting applies in the business world too. The life of both headhunter and jobseeker is rendered easier through neat packaging and differentiation. What you see is what you get; specialist expertise comes with a premium attached. Polymathic generalism is harder to categorise and reward.

Emilie Wapnick, advocate of multipotentiality, and her colleagues at Puttylike occasionally blog about the mental health effects that can result from living in more than one world. Wapnick's experiences are exacerbated by her own introversion and anxiety. These are not prerequisites for neo-generalism but they can certainly have a detrimental effect. As part of our research, we explored whether there was any correlation between introversion and generalism or extroversion and specialism. We could find none. Indeed, there was a wide array of introverts, ambiverts and extroverts among our neo-generalist interviewees. The authors themselves naturally incline towards opposite ends of the spectrum, although learned behaviours and context often bring each of them closer to the middle ground of ambiversion.

Wapnick's observations regarding the experience of imposter syndrome and its adverse effects, however, do ring true for many who have shared their stories with us. As Ella Saltmarshe argues, there is a need for the neo-generalist to maintain a balance between humility and confidence in themselves and their ideas. When the balance tips too far towards humility, however, self-doubt sets in and confidence in personal skills and experience is temporarily lost. Many confess that, in these low moments, they are waiting to be found out. They question their own expertise, their legitimacy to guide and influence others, their rootlessness and outsider perspective. Several admit to having experienced depression.

The nature of the neo-generalist means that they are constantly transforming. They move from one role to another, from one area of expertise to another, seeking relevance in new contexts. Sometimes, as Peter Vander Auwera suggests, they get trapped in a liminal state, in 'the zone between what was and what will become', seeking personal meaning and identity, not quite knowing in which direction to turn next. Like the trickster, many neo-generalists are shapeshifters, flexible, fluid and adaptive, but for some the frequent metamorphoses, the very diversity of what they are able to do, fragments their sense of identity.

As Herminia Ibarra argues in *Working Identity*, the evolutionary process of increasing our variety, of discovering and fleshing out our possible selves, creates fissures in the whole. Our self is in fact an assembly of selves. It is difficult to set down roots, to settle into a single character, if you are constantly on the move. There is a need to maintain an equilibrium between these different aspects, to recognise and nurture the whole, even while giving expression to the part. This is a struggle reflected in Joseph Campbell's monomyth, as well as in Abraham Maslow's notion of self-actualisation.

Intriguingly, many of our interviewees self-describe themselves as third-culture kids, children of immigrants or exiles who have elected to live in countries other than their birthplaces, often becoming dual citizens. This adds another dimension to the notion of juggling multiple identities. It requires cultural adjustment in some cases, and the integration of different nationalities and ethnicities in others. In many respects, such people are already polymathic, predisposed to the multidimensionality of neo-generalism. They are more than familiar with the mono-mythic journey, with integrating different aspects of their selves, having followed its path several times before.

In *Zen and the Art of Motorcycle Maintenance*, an early exploration of the specialist–generalist spectrum, Robert Pirsig comments on the distinction between physical and psychic distance. A person can be physically present, apparently part of an organisation, a community or culture. In reality, however, they feel far away, alienated, outsiders, temporary visitors. Even when recognised as a leader in their field, as is the case with Geoffrey West, for example, and his prominence among both theoretical physicists and biologists, there is no guarantee that they will ever develop a true sense of belonging. To align yourself fully with one field, one group, would deny the importance of the other domains in which you practise. Alienation is a regular theme in the stories we have heard. There is no guild for the neo-generalist. That skill set is too big, too broad, to accommodate in a single place.

Two different impulses can be in play here. First, there is the restlessness of the neo-generalist themselves. Their natural inquisitiveness pulls them towards new paths to investigate rather than the well-trodden routes. Sometimes they have no desire to belong, revelling in their outsider status, finding playful ways, radical ideas, with which to challenge and disrupt entrenched ways of thinking, doing and seeing. Always both/and, never either/or. Second, there is a lack of acceptance by the existing group, which mobilises its antibodies to deal with the foreign agent. Here the neo-generalist's otherness is viewed as a threat. The feeling of alienation then results from the attempts to exclude and eject. The trickster parallel is again illuminating here. The trickster can be viewed in a positive light as messenger, translator, border-crosser and catalyst to change. There is, however, a darker side to the archetype too, involving shapeshifting and mischief, that generates fear and mistrust. For some, the trickster is serial master, for others a con artist. That which is misunderstood is often rejected.

Connected to these notions of understanding and identity is the broad issue of diversity. It is a discussion that needs to extend beyond questions of gender, ethnicity, age and disability, although they all remain important. Diversity additionally needs to encompass ideas relating to mindset, educational background and experience. It is about plurality, about the blending of varied skills and capabilities. The former hotelier who joins the rail organisation may offer insights that would never occur to someone who has always worked in transportation. A health manager may bring something fresh to school administration, an engineer to the surgical operating theatre, a journalist to the corporate board, a chef to public health policy. It is not a case of disregarding what has been done before, but of adding new ingredients to the mix. It is thinking and acting at the edge of the box, pushing at the boundaries of creative constraint. Some of the difficulties the neo-generalist encounters in fitting in and being appreciated relate to the rigid industrial mindset's inability to appreciate the possibility and potential they offer.

The neo-generalist's tendency to wander can be fuelled by rejection and misunderstanding, by their own curiosity and desire to learn, by their entrepreneurial spirit, or simply by boredom. When you derive energy from the acquisition of knowledge and combinatory play, too much time spent doing the same thing can have an entropic effect. If your objective is to effect transformation, once that has been achieved it is the moment to move on to something different, passing the ball, handing over the jersey. In *Act Like a Leader, Think Like a Leader,* Herminia Ibarra's exploration of the leadership competency gap illustrates how individual preference, context and systemic constraint all service and promote specialism. The attributes she identifies to close this gap have many overlaps with the characteristics we have associated with neo-generalism.

The most successful leaders that Ibarra describes are WWW people, not T-shaped. They bridge from their teams, organisations and institutions to others, connecting the right ideas to the right people, leveraging the potential offered by the network. Their focus is on strategic development rather than executing operational requirements. They are able to envision possibilities and address big issues, whether at a local, corporate or societal level. Perhaps the alienation some of our neo-generalists admit to stems more from the loneliness of the leader, who always has to be on the move, traversing multiple worlds, stewarding the legacy?

Such stewardship requires that you recognise the opportunity for second curves, the need to step aside for new playmakers. Transformational leadership is followed by personal redundancy. To remain in place is, as Peter Vander Auwera recognises, to resign yourself to repetition and the ennui that accompanies it. In addition to many years of experience working at the innovative edges of the financial sector, Peter is also an artist. There comes a moment, he told us, when you know you have put the final brush stroke on your painting. The same applies when you know it is time to move on from a leadership role, time to change the business or discipline you dedicate your energy to, time to acknowledge that you are done and are heading once again down the path less travelled.

12.
FADE OUT

*It was always arcane knowledge
that we pursued; you know that now.
Early fascination with science had given
way to passions for magic and conjuring,
astrology, religion, contemporary poetry
in several languages, quantum theory,
the New Novel, Buddhism, obscure
music, obscure heroes.*

James Sallis, *Renderings*

When we travel on a bicycle, whether at speed or more sedately, we are constantly making minor adjustments, turning the handlebars, shifting our weight, in order to maintain equilibrium. Although learned consciously, this soon becomes entrenched in unconscious thought and muscle memory. It is rare that someone needs to relearn how to ride a bike. The rider adapts and responds to the curves in the road, the climbs and dips, the changes in the wind's direction. The mechanics of the body take over, and the mind is freed to focus on other things, tending to the seeds of new ideas, or navigating through rhizomatic pathways from root to blossom-filled branch as well-established concepts are explored anew. There exists a balance between the rider and the Earth's gravitational pull, just as there is between the body and the mind.

An unconscious equilibrium characterises the stories our interviewees have told us regarding their experiences as neo-generalists, finding balance on the curves and loops of specialism and generalism. It is unusual for someone to deliberately determine that today they will be a specialist, tomorrow a generalist. Most have evidenced a natural inclination towards, a preference for, the multidimensionality of the polymathic generalist. These people are, after all, lifelong learners, always interested in new ideas and their playful combination. But their idealistic inclinations tend to be leavened by a dose of realism, an acceptance that context will often require them to focus on narrow functional disciplines. After a time, they unthinkingly twist and dive across the curves of the neo-generalist continuum, only expressing discomfort when they find themselves trapped too long in a single specialism. Starved of new knowledge, new territory to wander, new discoveries to make, they lose their sense of balance.

Conceptually, neo-generalism is suggestive of holism rather than division. It unites polarised positions, bridging between them via a spectrum of subtle variations and hybridisations. It is a *meta* term applied to an expanding group of people whose own metaskills will be vital going forwards as mankind addresses the complex conundrums posed by environmental change, dwindling natural resources, advances in technology and healthcare, species longevity, military conflict, economic collapse and mass migration. These are people who can see not only the trees but the great forests of which they are part. They can contextualise the micro in terms of the macro, joining the fragments together not only to tell compelling stories but to bring together coalitions of other people from a variety of different disciplines to develop and apply solutions.

The neo-generalist dislikes labels and categorisation precisely because they have the effect of fragmenting and polarising, creating artificial boundaries and divisions. Separate schools of philosophical thought, different areas of working practice, develop their own technical languages. Communication breaks down as understanding is lost, and effectiveness all but disappears. It takes a trickster-like capability to infiltrate multiple communities and begin to translate between them. The neo-generalist serves as bridge and catalyst, perhaps never quite developing a true sense of belonging, but affecting change and establishing cooperative relationships between diverse fields. They bring too the ability to translate complex ideas into accessible language in order that it can be understood and acted upon by different audiences.

Moving around the continuum, in and out of different specialisms and responsibilities, working with an array of groups and communities, the neo-generalist lives in a state of perpetual beta. They are always becoming. This requires a level of comfort with ambiguity, with the not-known. But also self-awareness and self-understanding, as well as a willingness to reframe from the perspective of others too. They evolve and adapt as new knowledge and experience is acquired and blended with existing skills and capabilities. They are sensitive to contextual shifts, seeking opportunities even when tackling the most complex of problems. These are leadership qualities that the neo-generalist exercises in their capacity of playmaker, servant and teacher. A balance is found between learning oneself and facilitating and guiding the learning of others, of preparing the ground for future generations.

In Richard Linklater's film *Boyhood*, there is a scene in which Ethan Hawke's character reveals to his son that 'we're all just wingin' it'. This is a theme echoed in David Weinberger's 'In Over Our Heads', a commencement address he delivered at Simmons College in 2014. Throughout our early lives we talk about what we want to be when we grow up. Then middle age hits and there is the slow realisation and gradual acceptance that, actually, we never grow up. The potential, the opportunity, remains to be many things. To experiment and adapt. To appreciate that we are all imposters, and that there is nothing wrong with it.

Perhaps, with the neo-generalist, there is an understanding that we can never truly *know*, that all knowledge is ephemeral. There is no solitary niche into which we will fit while the blood remains pumping, the synapses crackling. We can go both broad and deep, bridging and eliding. We both learn and teach, listen and work out loud, collaborate and cooperate, lead and follow, give and take. Curiosity propels us, if we allow ourselves to maintain the wonder of a child, forever questioning. It is the page turner, opening up new chapters, enabling the acquisition of new knowledge, inviting new experiences, always leading us to the edge of what we know.

There is something about pushing the boundaries of knowledge that has the quality of a liminal state. Following curiosity is like wandering through a garden of forking paths, finding solace in the whole labyrinth and not just in the route taken. It is a process of endless transition – from not knowing to knowing and back to not knowing again. A shadow dance is played out through the mist, occasionally illuminated by a bright light. Knowledge enlightens and connects us to other people. Our relationships with others, our conversations with them, our exchange of learning and experience, all fuel our transitions, moving us from one state to another.

There is an aphorism in knowledge management circles that goes something like this: *We write less than we speak and know more than we say.* While there is a kernel of truth to this, it only hints at how personal knowledge actually is. We can make some of our knowledge visible through our actions, words, images or writing. We have shared it but it nevertheless remains our own, constrained by our context, our personal experience. Another person might consume some of what we have shared – observing, listening, reading – but they will make it their own, pass it through their own filters. Is that transference of knowledge? Not really. At best, we have helped catalyse their thought processes, possibly moved them to action, nothing more. Knowledge itself will remain personal. Separate it from the individual and their context, and it is questionable whether it is knowledge at all. Instead we are left with artefacts, information, data repositories, uncoupled from human experience and relationships.

Culturally, such ideas have a lineage that can be traced back to semiotics and structuralism. These schools of thought were indebted to the work of the linguist Ferdinand de Saussure. For him, the *sign* was the organising concept for all forms of language. A sign was comprised of two elements, the *signifier* and the *signified*. So, if someone were to say or write the word *cat* (signifier), a fellow Anglophone would infer from that a four-legged creature with a tail, pointy ears and whiskers (signified). Similarly, if they were to draw a sketch of such a creature (signifier), people would understand that they were alluding to a domestic pet that looked roughly the same (signified). The idea is beautifully captured in René Magritte's *The Treachery of Images* in which his painting of a pipe is accompanied by the words *Ceci n'est pas une pipe* (This is not a pipe). It is not a pipe because it is a picture of a pipe, a simulacrum.

Something similar happens with the exposure of our own knowledge. When we write it down or speak about it, we serve up a signifier. But our intentions may differ from the way another individual interprets what we write or say. They need to make it their own, assimilate it to their personal context, interpret it and use it in a manner that is unique to them. The ideas we share only become knowledge again when they have been internalised by someone else, made their own. The development of our neo-generalist argument, then, is a cooperative one. We have served up our current understanding of the topic and it is now up to you, the reader, to complete the thought, to make it your own.

This co-creative process is what the semiotician and novelist Umberto Eco termed *The Open Work*. There are authorial intentions packaged in any composition, but they are not restricted to a single interpretation. Other distinguished cultural producers and commentators like Milan Kundera (*The Art of the Novel*), Peter Turchi (*Maps of the Imagination*) and David Byrne (*How Music Works*) also highlight how the page, the frame, the stage, the lyric, the story and the canvas all serve as both a creative constraint and a bridge between artist and audience. There is a liminal space, an in-between, where meaning is made. Viewer by viewer, reader by reader, listener by listener, that interpretation, that personal *signified*, differs. There is no single truth but many variations.

In our view, the publication of a book is the beginning rather than the end. Alpha instead of Omega. It is an invitation to conversation. A call for constructive dialogue, challenge, agreement, critique. It is both the curse and the blessing of the neo-generalist to reject a single right answer. What we have offered here is nothing more than a contribution to the discussion. If it has succeeded in giving some readers a sense of identity, of belonging however tangentially to a broader community, of perhaps not being the oddity they once thought themselves to be, then all well and good. If it has persuaded others that the connective, big-picture capabilities of the neo-generalists should be valued alongside the deep expertise of specialists, then that gives us some cause for hope regarding the future. What we cannot offer you, however, is some neatly packaged, ribbon-tied conclusion.

If we disappoint the hedgehog by veering away from a single truth, perhaps we can satisfy the curiosity of the fox by supplying avenues to explore rather than answers. What follows are the questions that shaped the lengthy conversations with the interviewees for this book. These usually served as points of departure in wide-ranging discussions that ebbed and flowed between the personal and the macro, the master and the apprentice, the specialist and the generalist. These people were filled with an entrepreneurial spirit, effortless leadership qualities, an ability to guide and mentor, and an innate, never-sated thirst for knowledge. In short, they epitomised what we think of as *The Neo-Generalist*.

ROOTS AND BELONGING

As a child, what did you want to be when you grew up?

Do you have a clear image of what you want to do and achieve in your life today?

Is there a common denominator in the career choices you have made during your life?

How has multiculturalism influenced your life and career?

To which communities do you belong?

Have you encountered difficulties describing what you do to other people?

Why do you think we are so focused on tying labels to people?

Have you ever labelled yourself in order to be understood?

Have you ever withheld part of your repertoire in order to get your foot through the door?

What do you want your legacy to be?

SPECIALISM AND GENERALISM

What is a specialist?

What is a generalist?

What is the value of specialism and generalism?

Is there a difference in the way that a generalist and a specialist can stay relevant?

Do you have personal stories or metaphors that can describe what it is to be a specialist or a generalist?

Do you recognise, from your own experience, that there is a continuum between specialism and generalism?

Have you experienced the need to switch between specialism and generalism as context dictates?

What are the downsides to generalism?

LEARNING AND GUIDING

What is your impression of formal education?

Did formal education help or hinder you?

Does formal education favour the specialist or generalist in your view?

Do you think we will see a development towards specialism or generalism in the future of education?

How do you learn?

Have you experienced a master–apprenticeship relationship in your learning?

How important is social learning to you?

Do you think there is a difference between the way people with a generalist outlook learn compared to those with a specialist one?

What role does play have in the way that you work and learn? How do you hone your talent if you are good at more than one thing?

How do you use technology in order to connect with others, to learn, and in other aspects of your life?

If you had to design an approach to education fit for the twenty-first century, what would it look like?

FINAL REFLECTIONS

How do you live a life of meaning if you live in more than one world?

Are you a neo-generalist?

BIBLIOGRAPHY

*Read bibliographies.
It's not the book you start with,
it's the book that book leads you to.*

Austin Kleon, *Steal Like an Artist*

*Now I realized that not infrequently
books speak of books: it is as if they
spoke among themselves.*

Umberto Eco, *The Name of the Rose*

Abbas, Yasmine. *Le Néo-Nomadisme* (FYP éditions, 2011).

Alboher, Marci. *One Person/Multiple Careers: The Original Guide to the Slash Career* (HeyMarci, 2012).

Ardila, J. A. Garrido (ed.). *The Picaresque Novel in Western Literature: From the Sixteenth Century to the Neopicaresque* (Cambridge University Press, 2015).

Aristotle. *The Politics* (Penguin, 2000).

Auster, Paul. *The New York Trilogy* (Faber & Faber, 1988).

Badenhausen, Richard. *T. S. Eliot and the Art of Collaboration* (Cambridge University Press, 2004).

Bass, Jennifer, and Pat Kirkham. *Saul Bass: A Life in Film and Design* (Laurence King, 2011).

Bauby, Jean-Dominique. *The Diving-Bell and the Butterfly* (Harper Perennial, 2008).

Baudelaire, Charles. *Flowers of Evil* (Oxford Paperbacks, 2008).

Baudelaire, Charles. *The Painter of Modern Life* (Penguin, 2010).

Bayles, David, and Ted Orland. *Art and Fear: Observations on the Perils (and Rewards) of Artmaking* (Image Continuum Press, 2001).

Becker, Ernest. *The Birth and Death of Meaning: An Interdisciplinary Perspective on the Problem of Man* (Free Press, 1971, 2nd edition).

Benjamin, Walter. *The Work of Art in the Age of Mechanical Reproduction* (Penguin, 2008).

Bennis, Warren. *On Becoming a Leader* (Basic Books, 2009, 4th edition).

Bergkamp, Dennis, with David Winner. *Stillness and Speed: My Story* (Simon & Schuster, 2013).

Berlin, Isaiah. *The Hedgehog and the Fox: An Essay on Tolstoy's View of History* (Phoenix, 2014, 2nd edition).

Bock, Laszlo. *Work Rules! Insights from Inside Google That Will Transform How You Live and Lead* (John Murray, 2015).

Bolen, Jean Shinoda. *Goddesses in Everywoman: Powerful Archetypes in Women's Lives* (Harper, 2014).

Borges, Jorge Luis. *Collected Fictions* (Penguin, 1998).

Borges, Jorge Luis. *Selected Poems* (Penguin, 2000).

Bowles, Paul. *Travels: Collected Writings, 1950-1993* (Ecco Press, 2011).

Boynton, Andy, and Bill Fischer. *Virtuoso Teams: Lessons from Teams That Changed Their Worlds* (Financial Times/Prentice Hall, 2005).

Brafman, Ori, and Rod A. Beckstrom. *The Starfish and the Spider: The Unstoppable Power of Leaderless Organizations* (Portfolio, 2007).

Brafman, Ori, and Judah Pollack. *The Chaos Imperative: How Chance and Disruption Increase Innovation, Effectiveness, and Success* (Piatkus, 2013).

Broadbridge, Edward, Clay Warren, and Uffe Jonas. *School for Life: N. F. S. Grundtvig on the Education for the People* (Aarhus University, 2012).

Brooks, David. *The Road to Character* (Allen Lane, 215).

Brown, Tim. *Change by Design: How Design Thinking Transforms Organizations and Inspires Innovation* (HarperBusiness, 2009).

Brown, Valerie A., John A. Harris and Jacqueline Y. Russell. *Tackling Wicked Problems: Through the Transdisciplinary Imagination* (Earthscan, 2010).

Bruford, Walter Horace. *The German Tradition of Self-Cultivation: Bildung from Humboldt to Thomas Mann* (Cambridge University Press, 1975).

Byrne, David. *Bicycle Diaries* (Faber & Faber, 2009).

Byrne, David. *How Music Works* (Canongate, 2013).

Cain, Susan. *Quiet: The Power of Introverts in a World That Can't Stop Talking* (Penguin, 2012).

Caldicott, Sarah Miller. *Midnight Lunch: The 4 Phases of Team Collaboration Success from Thomas Edison's Lab* (Wiley, 2013).

Calvino, Italo. *Six Memos for the Next Millennium* (Penguin, 2009).

Campbell, Joseph. *The Hero with a Thousand Faces* (New World Library, 2012, 3rd edition).

Carr, Edward. 'The Last Days of the Polymath', *Intelligent Life* (Autumn 2009). http://moreintelligentlife.com/content/edward-carr/last-days-polymath.

Carr, Nicholas. *The Shallows: What the Internet Is Doing to Our Brains* (W. W. Norton, 2011).

Castaneda, Carlos. *The Teachings of Don Juan: A Yaqui Way of Knowledge* (Penguin, 2004).

Catmull, Ed, with Amy Wallace. *Creativity, Inc.: Overcoming the Unseen Forces That Stand in the Way of True Inspiration* (Bantam Press, 2014).

Cawelti, John G. *Adventure, Mystery, and Romance: Formula Stories as Art and Popular Culture* (University of Chicago Press, 1977).

Chabon, Michael. *Maps and Legends: Reading and Writing Along the Borderlands* (Fourth Estate, 2010).

Chase, Robin. *Peers Inc: How People and Platforms Are Inventing the Collaborative Economy and Reinventing Capitalism* (Headline, 2015).

Clark, Glenn. *The Man Who Tapped the Secrets of the Universe* (Filiquarian Publishing, 2007).

Colegrave, Stephen, and Chris Sullivan. *Punk: A Life Apart* (Cassell, 2004).

Cooke, Nicole. *The Breakaway: My Story* (Simon & Schuster, 2014).

Coverley, Merlin. *The Art of Wandering* (Oldcastle Books, 2012).

Cruickshank, Dan. *Bridges: Heroic Designs that Changed the World* (Collins, 2010).

Crumey, Andrew. *Mobius Dick* (Picador, 2005).

Csikszentmihalyi, Mihaly. *Beyond Boredom and Anxiety: Experiencing Flow in Work and Play* (John Wiley & Sons, 2000).

Csikszentmihalyi, Mihaly. *Creativity: Flow and the Psychology of Discovery and Invention* (Harper Perennial, 2013).

Csikszentmihalyi, Mihaly. *Flow: The Psychology of Happiness* (Rider, 2002).

Cummings, E. E. *Selected Poems, 1923-1958* (Faber & Faber, 1977).

Dahl, Roald. *Charlie and the Chocolate Factory* (Puffin, 2005).

Darling, Lynn. *Out of the Woods: A Memoir of Wayfinding* (Harper Perennial, 2015).

Das, Gurcharan. *The Difficulty of Being Good: On the Subtle Art of Dharma* (Oxford University Press, 2010).

Davenport, Thomas H. *Thinking for a Living: How to Get Better Performance and Results from Knowledge Workers* (Harvard Business School Press, 2005).

de Beauvoir, Simone. *The Ethics of Ambiguity* (Philosophical Library, 2015).

de Bono, Edward. *Six Thinking Hats* (Back Bay Books, 1999).

de Botton, Alain, and John Armstrong. *Art as Therapy* (Phaeton, 2013).

de Cervantes, Miguel. *Don Quixote* (Secker & Warburg, 2004).

Dehnugara, Khurshed. *Flawed but Willing: Leading Organisations in the Age of Connection* (LID, 2014).

De La Pava, Sergio. *A Naked Singularity* (MacLehose Press, 2013).

DeLillo, Don. *Underworld* (Picador, 1999).

DeLillo, Don. *White Noise* (Picador, 1999).

DeLong, David W. *Lost Knowledge: Confronting the Threat of an Aging Workforce* (Oxford University Press, 2004).

Deutsch, David. *The Beginning of Infinity: Explanations that Transform the World* (Penguin, 2011).

Dewey, John. *Democracy and Education* (Benediction Books, 2011).

Didau, David. *What If Everything You Knew About Education Was Wrong?* (Crown House, 2015).

Doane, Randall. *Stealing All Transmissions: A Secret History of The Clash* (PM Press, 2014).

Douglas, Thomas, and John Seely Brown. *A New Culture of Learning* (CreateSpace Independent Publishing Platform, 2011).

Dreyfus, Hubert, and Sean Dorrance Kelly. *All Things Shining: Reading the Western Classics to Find Meaning in a Secular Age* (Free Press, 2011).

Drucker, Peter F. *Management Challenges for the 21st Century* (Harper Business, 2001).

Drucker, Peter F. *Managing Oneself* (Harvard Business School Press, 2008).

D'Souza, Steven, and Diana Renner. *Not Knowing: The Art of Turning Uncertainty into Opportunity* (LID, 2014).

Dweck, Carol. *Mindset: How You Can Fulfill Your Potential* (Robinson, 2012).

Dyer, Geoff. *The Search* (Penguin, 1995).

Earls, Mark. *Herd: How to Change Mass Behaviour by Harnessing Our True Nature* (Wiley, 2009).

Eckō, Marc. *Unlabel: Selling You Without Selling Out* (Touchstone, 2013).

Eco, Umberto. *The Name of the Rose* (Picador, 1984).

Eco, Umberto. *The Open Work* (Harvard University Press, 1989).

Eco, Umberto. *Reflections on The Name of the Rose* (Secker & Warburg, 1985).

Egan, Gerard. *The Skilled Helper: A Problem-Management and Opportunity-Development Approach to Helping* (Wadsworth Publishing, 2001, 7th edition).

Einstein, Albert. *Ideas and Opinions* (Souvenir Press, 2005).

Einstein, Albert. *The World As I See It* (Citadel Press, 2006).

Eliot, T. S. *The Poems of T. S. Eliot, Volumes I & II* (Faber & Faber, 2015).

Fitzgerald, F. Scott. 'The Crack-up', *Esquire* (February–April 1936). http://www.esquire.com/news-politics/a4310/the-crack-up/.

Frayling, Christopher. *On Craftsmanship: Towards a New Bauhaus* (Oberon Books, 2011).

Fredens, Kjeld. *Innovation and Leadership* (Gyldendal, 2009).

Fuller, R. Buckminster. *Synergetics: Explorations in the Geometry of Thinking* (Macmillan, 1979).

Gardner, Howard. *Five Minds for the Future* (Harvard Business School Press, 2007).

Gardner, John W. *Self-Renewal: The Individual and the Innovative Society* (W. W. Norton, 1963).

Garfield, Simon. *On The Map: Why the World Looks the Way It Does* (Profile Books, 2012).

Gawande, Atul. *The Checklist Manifesto: How to Get Things Right* (Profile Books, 2010).

Gelb, Michael J., and Sarah Miller Caldicott. *Innovate Like Edison* (Dutton Books, 2007).

Gimpel, Jean. *The Cathedral Builders* (Evergreen Books, 1961).

Gladwell, Malcolm. *Outliers* (Little, Brown, 2008).

Gladwell, Malcolm. *The Tipping Point* (Abacus, 2013).

Gleick, James. *The Information: A History, a Theory, a Flood* (Fourth Estate, 2011).

Gleiser, Marcelo. *The Island of Knowledge: The Limits of Science and the Seach for Meaning* (Basic Books, 2014).

Godin, Seth. *Tribes: We Need You to Lead Us* (Portfolio, 2008).

Gomez, Peter, and Timo Meynhardt. 'More Foxes in the Boardroom: Systems Thinking in Action', in Stefan N. Grösser and René Zeir (eds.), *Systemic Management for Intelligent Organizations: Concepts, Model-Based Approaches and Application* (Springer, 2012).

Gorbis, Marina. *The Nature of the Future: Dispatches from the Socialstructed World* (Free Press, 2013).

Gould, Stephen Jay. *The Hedgehog, the Fox, and the Magister's Pox: Mending and Minding the Misconceived Gap Between Science and the Humanities* (Vintage, 2004).

Grant, Adam. *Give and Take: A Revolutionary Approach to Success* (Viking Books, 2013).

Grant, Adam. *Originals: How Non-Conformists Change the World* (W. H. Allen, 2016).

Gratton, Lynda. *The Shift: The Future of Work is Already Here* (William Collins, 2014).

Gray, Dave, with Thomas Vander Wal. *The Connected Company* (O'Reilly, 2012).

Grayling, A. C. *The Challenge of Things: Thinking Through Troubled Times* (Bloomsbury, 2015).

Grazer, Brian, and Charles Fishman. *A Curious Mind: The Secret to a Bigger Life* (Simon & Schuster, 2015).

Gros, Frédéric. *A Philosophy of Walking* (Verso, 2015).

Grosz, Stephen. *The Examined Life: How We Lose and Find Ourselves* (Vintage, 2014).

Habermas, Jürgen. *The Theory of Communicative Action, Volume 1: Reason and the Rationalisation of Society* (Beacon Press, 1985).

Habermas, Jürgen. *The Theory of Communicative Action, Volume 2: Lifeworld and System: A Critique of Functionalist Reason* (Beacon Press, 1985).

Hagel, John, John Seely Brown and Lang Davidson. *The Power of Pull: How Small Moves, Smartly Made, Can Set Big Things in Motion* (Basic Books, 2010).

Hagy, Jessica. *How To Be Interesting* (Workman, 2013).

Hall, Donald. *Life Work* (Beacon Press, 2003).

Halpern, Paul. *Einstein's Dice and Schrödinger's Cat: How Two Great Minds Battled Quantum Randomness to Create a Unified Theory of Physics* (Basic Books, 2015).

Handy, Charles. *The Age of Unreason* (Arrow, 2002).

Handy, Charles. *The Elephant and the Flea* (Arrow, 2002).

Handy, Charles. *The Empty Raincoat* (Arrow, 2002).

Handy, Charles. *Myself and Other More Important Matters* (Arrow, 2007).

Handy, Charles. *The Second Curve: Thoughts on Reinventing Society* (Random House, 2015).

Hansen, Morten T., and Bolko von Oetinger. 'Introducing T-Shaped Managers: Knowledge Management's Next Generation', *Harvard Business Review* (March 2001).

Hansen, Morten T. *Collaboration: How Leaders Avoid the Traps, Build Common Ground, and Reap Big Results* (Harvard Business Review Press, 2009).

Harari, Yuval Noah. *Sapiens: A Brief History of Humankind* (Vintage, 2015).

Hardy, Steve. *The Creative Generalist* (ChangeThis, 2005). http://changethis.com/manifesto/show/19.CreativeGeneralist.

Hargadon, Andrew. *How Breakthroughs Happen: The Surprising Truth About How Companies Innovate* (Harvard Business School Press, 2003).

Harford, Tim. *Adapt: Why Success Always Starts with Failure* (Abacus, 2012).

Haultain, Arnold. *Of Walks and Walking Tours: An Attempt to find a Philosophy and a Creed* (HardPress, 2015).

Heath, Chip, and Dan Heath. *Switch: How to Change Things When Change is Hard* (Random House, 2011).

Heidegger, Martin. *The Question Concerning Technology and Other Essays* (Harper Perennial, 2013).

Heisenberg, Werner. *Physics and Philosophy: The Revolution in Modern Science* (Penguin, 2000).

Hemingway, Ernest. *A Moveable Feast* (Scribner, 2010).

Hidalgo, César. *Why Information Grows: The Evolution of Order, from Atoms to Economies* (Allen Lane, 2015).

Hitchens, Christopher. *Hitch-22: A Memoir* (Atlantic Books, 2011).

Holmes, Jamie. *Nonsense: The Power of Not Knowing* (Crown, 2015).

Horowitz, Alexandra. *On Looking: A Walker's Guide to the Art of Observation* (Scribner, 2013).

Hoque, Faisal, with Drake Baer. *Everything Connects: How to Transform and Lead in the Age of Creativity, Innovation, and Sustainability* (McGraw-Hill, 2014).

Hutchens, David. *Circle of the 9 Muses: A Storytelling Field Guide for Innovators and Meaning Makers* (Wiley, 2015).

Hyde, Lewis. *Trickster Makes This World: How Disruptive Imagination Creates Culture* (Canongate, 2008).

Hytner, Richard. *Consiglieri: Leading from the Shadows* (Profile Books, 2014).

Ibarra, Herminia. *Act Like a Leader, Think Like a Leader* (Harvard Business School Press, 2015).

Ibarra, Herminia. *Working Identity: Unconventional Strategies for Reinventing Your Career* (Harvard Business School Press, 2004).

Ilves, Erika, and Anna Stillwell. *The Human Project* (The Human Project, 2013).

Isaacson, Walter. *Steve Jobs* (Little, Brown, 2011).

Iyer, Pico. *The Art of Stillness: Adventures in Going Nowhere* (Simon & Schuster/TED, 2014).

Jackson, Kevin. *Constellation of Genius – 1922: Modernism and All That Jazz* (Windmill Books, 2013).

Jacobs, Michael. *Between Hopes and Memories: A Spanish Journey* (Picador, 1996).

Jarche, Harold. *Adapting to Perpetual Beta* (Tantramar Interactive, 2015).

Jarche, Harold. *Finding Perpetual Beta* (Tantramar Interactive, 2014).

Jarche, Harold. *Seeking Perpetual Beta* (Tantramar Interactive, 2014).

Jensen, Rolf, and Mika Aaltonen. *The Renaissance Society: How the Shift from Dream Society to the Age of Individual Control Will Change the Way You Do Business* (McGraw-Hill, 2013).

Johnson, Steven. *How We Got to Now: Six Innovations that Made the Modern World* (Particular Books, 2014).

Johnson, Steven. *Where Good Ideas Come From: The Seven Patterns of Innovation* (Penguin, 2011).

Jones, Wendy. *Grayson Perry: Portrait of the Artist as a Young Girl* (Vintage, 2007).

Kakko, Ilkka. *Oasis Way and the Post-Normal Era: How Understanding Serendipity Will Lead You To Success* (BHV-Petersburg, 2014).

Kaipa, Prasad, and Navi Radjou. *From Smart to Wise: Acting and Leading with Wisdom* (Jossey-Bass, 2013).

Kahneman, Daniel. *Thinking, Fast and Slow* (Penguin, 2012).

Kawin, Bruce F. *Mindscreen: Bergman, Godard, and First-Person Film* (Princeton University Press, 1978).

Kay, John. *Obliquity: Why Our Goals Are Best Achieved Indirectly* (Profile Books, 2010).

Kegan, Robert. *Immunity to Change: How to Overcome It and Unlock the Potential in Yourself and Your Organization* (Harvard Business School Press, 2009).

Kellerman, Barbara. *The End of Leadership* (HarperBusiness, 2012).

Kellert, Stephen H. *Borrowed Knowledge: Chaos Theory and the Challenge of Learning Across Disciplines* (University of Chicago Press, 2008).

Kelley, David, and Tom Kelley. *Creative Confidence: Unleashing the Creative Potential Within Us All* (William Collins, 2013).

Kelley, Tom. *The Ten Faces of Innovation: IDEO's Strategies for Defeating the Devil's Advocate and Driving Creativity Throughout Your Organization* (Currency/Doubleday, 2005).

Kennedy, John F. 'Remarks Prepared for Delivery at the Trade Mart in Dallas, TX' (22 November 1963). http://www.jfklibrary.org/Research/Research-Aids/JFK-Speeches/Dallas-TX-Trade-Mart-Undelivered_19631122.aspx

Kerr, James. *Legacy: 15 Lessons in Leadership* (Constable, 2013).

Kilpi, Esko. 'Complex Intelligence', *Medium* (February 2016). https://medium.com/@EskoKilpi/complex-intelligence-21f7908f3c23#.g8y82trjp

Kirkeby, Ole Fogh. *The New Protreptic: The Concept and the Art* (Copenhagen Business School Press DK, 2009).

Kirkeby, Ole Fogh. *The Virtue of Leadership* (Copenhagen Business School Press DK, 2008).

Klein, Gary. *Seeing What Others Don't: The Remarkable Ways We Gain Insights* (Nicholas Brealey, 2014).

Klein, Jacky. *Grayson Perry* (Thames & Hudson, 2013).

Kleon, Austin. *Show Your Work! 10 Ways to Share Your Creativity and Get Discovered* (Workman, 2014).

Kleon, Austin. *Steal Like An Artist: 10 Things Nobody Told You About Being Creative* (Workman, 2012).

Krznaric, Roman. *Empathy: A Handbook for Revolution* (Rider, 2014).

Krznaric, Roman. *How to Find Fulfilling Work* (Macmillan, 2012).

Krznaric, Roman. *The Wonderbox: Curious Histories of How to Live* (Profile Books, 2011).

Kundera, Milan. *The Art of the Novel* (Faber & Faber, 1999).

Kundera, Milan. *The Curtain: An Essay in Seven Parts* (Faber & Faber, 2007).

Kundera, Milan. *The Unbearable Lightness of Being* (Faber & Faber, 1985).

Laloux, Frédéric. *Reinventing Organizations: A Guide to Creating Organizations Inspired by the Next Stage in Human Consciousness* (Nelson Parker, 2014).

Leatherdale, Clive. *The Book of Football: A Complete History and Record of the Association and Rugby Games, 1905-06* (Desert Island Books, 2005).

Leslie, Ian. *Curious: The Desire to Know and Why Your Future Depends On It* (Quercus, 2014).

Levine, Rick, Christopher Locke, Doc Searls and David Weinberger. *The Cluetrain Manifesto: The End of Business as Usual* (Basic Books, 2011).

Levitin, Daniel J. *The Organized Mind: Thinking Straight in the Age of Information Overload* (Penguin, 2015).

Lewis, Michael. *Moneyball: The Art of Winning an Unfair Game* (W. W. Norton, 2004).

Liao, Bill. *Forests: Reasons to be Hopeful* (Ideos, 2013).

Liao, Bill. *Stone Soup: The Secret Recipe for Making Something from Nothing* (Bookshaker, 2010).

Lobenstine, Margaret. *The Renaissance Soul: Life Design for People with Too Many Passions to Pick Just One* (Broadway Books, 2006).

Løgstrup, Knud Ejler. *The Ethical Demand* (University of Notre Dame Press, 1997).

MacKenzie, Gordon. *Orbiting the Giant Hairball: A Corporate Fool's Guide to Surviving with Grace* (Viking Penguin, 1998).

Maeda, John. *Redesigning Leadership* (MIT Press, 2011).

Makimoto, Tsugio, and David Manners. *Digital Nomad* (Wiley, 1997).

Malnight, Thomas, Tracey Keys and Kees van der Graaf. *Ready? The 3Rs of Preparing Your Organization for the Future* (Strategy Dynamics Global SA, 2013).

Malone, Thomas W., Robert Launcher and Tammy Johns. 'The Big Idea: The Age of Hyperspecialization', *Harvard Business Review* (July-August 2011). https://hbr.org/2011/07/the-big-idea-the-age-of-hyperspecialization.

Mansharamani, Vikram. 'All Hail the Generalist', *Harvard Business Review Blog* (June 2012). https://hbr.org/2012/06/all-hail-the-generalist.

Markman, Art. 'Picasso, Kepler, and the Benefits of Being an Expert Generalist', 99u (January 2013). http://99u.com/articles/7269/Picasso-Kepler-and-the-Benefits-of-Being-an-Expert-Generalist.

Márquez, Gabriel García. *One Hundred Years of Solitude* (Penguin, 1972).

Martin, Gerald. *Journeys Through the Labyrinth: Latin American Fiction in the Twentieth Century* (Verso, 1989).

Martin, Richard. *Mean Streets and Raging Bulls: The Legacy of Film Noir in Contemporary American Cinema* (Scarecrow Press, 1997).

Martin, Richard. 'Memories of Things Past and Yet to Come: James Sallis, Allusionism, and Play', *Crime Time* 2.4 (1999). http://jamessallis.com/martin.html

Martin, Roger L. *The Opposable Mind: Winning Through Integrative Thinking* (Harvard Business Press, 2009).

Mathews, Adrian. *The Hat of Victor Noir* (Fourth Estate, 1996).

McGowan, Todd. *The Fictional Christopher Nolan* (University of Texas Press, 2012).

Meadows, Donella H. *Thinking in Systems: A Primer* (Chelsea Green Publishing, 2008).

Messina, Chris. 'The Full-Stack Employee', *Medium* (April 2015). https://medium.com/chris-messina/the-full-stack-employee-ed0db089f0a1#.3e4nqaywc

Meynhardt, Timo, Carolin Hermann and Stefan Anderer. 'Do You Think Like a Hedgehog or a Fox?', *Dialogue* 8 (June–August 2015).

Mikkelsen, Kenneth. 'Do You Take the Blue Pill or the Red Pill?', *Drucker Society Europe* (February 2015). http://www.druckerforum.org/blog/?p=766.

Mikkelsen, Kenneth, and Harold Jarche. 'The Best Leaders Are Constant Learners', *Harvard Business Review* (October 2015). https://hbr.org/2015/10/the-best-leaders-are-constant-learners

Miller, Arthur I. *Einstein, Picasso: Space, Time, and the Beauty That Causes Havoc* (Basic Books, 2001).

Mirchandani, Vinnie. *The New Polymath: Profiles in Compound-Technology Innovations* (Wiley, 2010).

Moore, Alan. *No Straight Lines: Making Sense of Our Non-Linear World* (Bloodstone Books, 2011).

Moravec, John W. (ed.). *Knowmad Society* (Education Futures, 2013).

Morville, Peter. *Intertwingled: Information Changes Everything* (Semantic Studios, 2014).

Neumeier, Marty. *Metaskills: Five Talents for the Robotic Age* (New Riders, 2013).

Nussbaum, Bruce. *Creative Intelligence: Harnessing the Power to Create, Connect, and Inspire* (HarperBusiness, 2013).

Nussbaum, Martha C. *Creating Capabilities: The Human Development Approach* (Harvard University Press, 2011).

Ortega y Gasset, José. *The Dehumanization of Art and Other Essays on Art, Culture, and Literature* (Princeton University Press, 1968).

Pagel, Mark. *Wired for Culture: The Natural History of Human Cooperation* (Penguin, 2013).

Palmer, Amanda. *The Art of Asking: or How I Learned to Stop Worrying and Let People Help* (Piatkus, 2014).

Perry, Grayson. *Playing to the Gallery: Helping Contemporary Art in Its Struggle to Be Understood* (Particular Books, 2014).

Perry, Grayson. 'The Rise and Fall of Default Man', *The New Statesman* (October 2014).

Pfeffer, Jeffrey, and Robert I. Sutton. *The Knowing-Doing Gap: How Smart Companies Turn Knowledge into Action* (Harvard Business School Press, 1999).

Phillips, Thomas. *Liminal Fictions in Postmodern Culture: The Politics of Self-Development* (Palgrave Macmillan, 2015).

Pink, Daniel H. *A Whole New Mind: Why Right-Brainers Will Rule the Future* (Riverhead Books, 2005).

Pink, Daniel H. *Drive: The Surprising Truth About What Motivates Us* (Canongate Books, 2013).

Pink, Daniel H. *To Sell is Human: The Surprising Truth About Persuading, Convincing, and Influencing Others* (Canongate Books, 2014).

Pirsig, Robert M. *Zen and the Art of Motorcycle Maintenance: An Inquiry into Values* (Vintage, 2004).

Popova, Maria. 'How Einstein Thought: Why *Combinatory Play* Is the Secret of Genius', *Brain Pickings* (August 2013). https://www.brainpickings.org/2013/08/14/how-einstein-thought-combinatorial-creativity/

Popova, Maria. 'Networked Knowledge and Combinatorial Creativity', *Brain Pickings* (August 2011). https://www.brainpickings.org/index.php/2011/08/01/networked-knowledge-combinatorial-creativity/

Pontefract, Dan. *The Purpose Effect: Building Meaning in Yourself, Your Role, and Your Organization* (Elevate, 2016).

Powell, Michael. *Million-Dollar Movie* (Heinemann, 1992).

Prehn, Anette, and Kjeld Fredens. *Play Your Brain: Adopt a Musical Mindset and Change Your Life and Career* (Marshall Cavendish Business, 2011).

Price, David. *Open: How We'll Work, Live and Learn in the Future* (Crux, 2013).

Putnam, Robert D. *Bowling Alone: The Collapse and Revival of American Community* (Simon & Schuster, 2001).

Pynchon, Thomas. *Bleeding Edge* (Vintage, 2014).

Pynchon, Thomas. *The Crying of Lot 49* (Pan, 1979).

Rehn, Alf. *Dangerous Ideas: When Provocative Thinking Is Your Most Valuable Asset* (BookBaby, 2013).

Rhodes, Richard. *Hedy's Folly: The Life and Breakthrough Inventions of Hedy Lamarr, the Most Beautiful Woman in the World* (Doubleday, 2012).

Robb, Graham. *The Discovery of France* (Picador, 2007).

Robb, Graham. *Parisians: An Adventure History of Paris* (Picador, 2010).

Robinson, Ken. *Out of Our Minds: Learning to Be Creative* (Capstone, 2011, revised and updated edition).

Robinson, Simon, and Maria Moraes Robinson. *Holonomics: Business Where People and Planet Matter* (Floris Books, 2014).

Roe, Sue. *In Montmartre: Picasso, Matisse and Modernism in Paris, 1900-1910* (Penguin, 2014).

Roosevelt, Eleanor. *You Learn by Living: Eleven Keys for a More Fulfilling Life* (Harper Perennial, 2012).

Ross, Alec. *The Industries of the Future* (Simon & Schuster, 2016).

Roszak, Theodore. *Flicker* (Bantam, 1992).

Rulfo, Juan. *Pedro Páramo* (Serpent's Tail, 1994).

Rushkoff, Douglas. *Present Shock: When Everything Happens Now* (Current, 2013).

Sallis, James. *Death Will Have Your Eyes* (No Exit Press, 1997).

Sallis, James. *Gently into the Land of the Meateaters* (Black Heron Press, 2000).

Sallis, James. *Renderings* (Black Heron Press, 1995).

Sanders, Ian. *On Being Curious* (Amazon Media, 2013).

Sanders, Ian, and David Sloly. *Mash-up! How to Use Your Multiple Skills to Give You an Edge, Make Money and Be Happier* (Kogan Page, 2012).

Sayer, Andrew. *Why Things Matter to People: Social Science, Values and Ethical Life* (Cambridge University Press, 2011).

Scott, Robyn. 'The Power of Quiet Connectors', *Medium* (October 2013). https://medium.com/@robynscott/the-power-of-quiet-connectors-7bc355c7f31b#.c1qlvtl1s

Schultz, Kathryn. *Being Wrong: Adventures in the Margin of Error* (Portobello Books, 2011).

Seaton, Matt. 'The Wanderer', *Rouleur* 58 (2015).

Semple, Euan. *Organizations Don't Tweet, People Do: A Manager's Guide to the Social Web* (Wiley, 2012).

Sennett, Richard. *The Craftsman* (Penguin, 2009).

Shakespeare, William. *The RSC Shakespeare: The Complete Works* (Macmillan, 2008).

Shaughnessy, Haydn. *Shift: A User's Guide to the New Economy* (Tru Publishing, 2015).

Shenk, Joshua Wolf. *Powers of Two: Finding the Essence of Innovation in Creative Pairs* (John Murray, 2014).

Silver, Nate. 'What the Fox Knows', *FiveThirtyEight* (March 2014). http://fivethirtyeight.com/features/what-the-fox-knows/

Singh, Simon. *The Code Book: The Secret History of Codes and Code-breaking* (Fourth Estate, 2010).

Smith, Keri. *How to Be an Explorer of the World* (Penguin, 2011).

Smith, Paul. *You Can Find Inspiration in Everything (And If You Can't, Look Again)* (Thames & Hudson, 2003).

Sousanis, Nick. *Unflattening* (Harvard University Press, 2015).

Spalding, Steven, and James Gibson. *Rebuilding the Polymath: And Other Insights Into the World of Innovation* (Project Mona, 2013).

Stadil, Christian, and Lene Tanggaard. *In the Shower with Picasso: Sparking Your Creativity and Imagination* (LID, 2014).

Stepper, John. *Working Out Loud: For a Better Career and Life* (Ikigai Press, 2015).

Stewart, Matthew. *The Management Myth: Why the Experts Keep Getting it Wrong* (W. W. Norton, 2009).

Sulloway, Frank J. *Born to Rebel: Birth Order, Family Dynamics, and Creative Lives* (Vintage, 1997).

Surowiecki, James. *The Wisdom of Crowds: Why the Many Are Smarter Than the Few* (Abacus, 2005).

Susskind, Richard, and Daniel Susskind. *The Future of Professions: How Technology Will Transform the Work of Human Experts* (Oxford University Press, 2015).

Taleb, Nicholas Nassim. *Antifragile: Things that Gain from Disorder* (Penguin, 2013).

Taleb, Nicholas Nassim. *The Black Swan: The Impact of the Highly Improbable* (Penguin, 2010).

Tartt, Donna. *The Goldfinch* (Abacus, 2014).

Tester, Keith (ed.). *The Flâneur* (Routledge, 1994).

Tetlock, Philip E. *Expert Political Judgment: How Good Is it? How Can We Know?* (Princeton University Press, 2005).

Tetlock, Philip E., and Dan Gardner. *Superforecasting: The Art and Science of Prediction* (Random House, 2015).

Tett, Gillian. *The Silo Effect: Why Putting Everything in its Place Isn't Such a Bright Idea* (Little, Brown, 2015).

Thompson, Jon. *Fiction, Crime, and Empire: Clues to Modernity and Postmodernism* (University of Illinois Press, 1993).

Thompson, Robert J. *Television's Second Golden Age: From Hill Street Blues to ER* (Syracuse University Press, 1996).

Turchi, Peter. *Maps of the Imagination: The Writer as Cartographer* (Trinity University Press, 2004).

Turchi, Peter. *A Muse and A Maze: Writing as Puzzle, Mystery, and Magic* (Trinity University Press, 2014).

Turkle, Sherry. *Alone Together: Why We Expect More From Technology and Less From Each Other* (Basic Books, 2011).

Turkle, Sherry. *Reclaiming Conversation: The Power of Talk in a Digital Age* (Penguin, 2015).

Twigger, Robert. 'Master of Many Trades', *Aeon* (November 2013). https://aeon.co/essays/we-live-in-a-one-track-world-but-anyone-can-become-a-polymath

Tzu, Lao. *Tao Te Ching* (Vintage, 2011, 3rd edition).

Vitalari, Nicholas, and Haydn Shaughnessy. *The Elastic Enterprise: The New Manifesto for Business Revolution* (Telemachus Press, 2012).

Vygotsky, Lev Semyonovich. *Mind in Society: Development of Higher Psychological Processes* (Harvard University Press, 1978).

Wagner, Tony. *Creating Innovators: The Making of Young People Who Will Change the World* (Scribner, 2014).

Wapnick, Emilie. *The 'Undeclared for Life' Manifesto: A Plan of Attack for the Person with Many Interests and Creative Pursuits* (Puttylike, 2010).

Watt, James. *Business for Punks: Break All the Rules – The BrewDog Way* (Portfolio Penguin, 2015).

Weinberger, David. 'In Over Our Heads', *Medium* (May 2014). https://medium.com/@dweinberger/in-over-our-heads-5ee8067bdac7#.z7qfit4qj.

Weinberger, David. *Small Pieces Loosely Joined: A Unified Theory of the Web* (Basic Books, 2003).

Weinberger, David. *Too Big to Know* (Basic Books, 2012).

Weinstein, Arnold. 'Don't Turn Away from the Art of Life', *The New York Times* (23 February 2016). http://www.nytimes.com/2016/02/24/opinion/dont-turn-away-from-the-art-of-life.html

Weiss, Philip. *HyperThinking: Creating a New Mindset for the Age of Networks* (Gower, 2012).

Weiwei, Ai, and Anthony Pins (eds.). *Ai Weiwei: Spatial Matters: Art, Architecture and Activism* (Tate Publishing, 2014).

Westwood, Vivienne, and Ian Kelly. *Vivienne Westwood* (Picador, 2014).

Wheatley, Margaret J. *Finding Our Way: Leadership for an Uncertain Time* (Berrett-Koehler Publishers, 2007).

White, Edmund. *The Flâneur: A Stroll through the Paradoxes of Paris* (Bloomsbury, 2015).

White, Kit. *101 Things to Learn in Art School* (MIT Press, 2011).

Whitman, Walt. *The Complete Poems* (Penguin, 2004).

Whyte, David. *Pilgrim* (Many Rivers Press, 2014, second edition).

Whyte, David. *River Flow: New and Selected Poems* (Many Rivers Press, 2012).

Whyte, David. *Three Marriages: Reimagining Work, Self and Relationship* (Riverhead Books, 2010).

Williams, Richard. *The Perfect 10: Football's Dreamers, Schemers, Playmakers and Playboys* (Faber & Faber, 2006).

Wilson, Edward O. *Consilience: The Unity of Knowledge* (Vintage, 1999).

Wilson, Edward O. *The Meaning of Human Existence* (Liveright, 2014).

Wilson, Jonathan. *The Outsider: A History of the Goalkeeper* (Orion, 2012).

Wilson, Richard, with Matthew Kálmán Mezey and Nick Nielsen. *Anti Hero: The Hidden Revolution in Leadership and Change* (Osca Agency, 2013).

Woodward, Clive. *Winning!* (Hodder, 2004).

Zakaria, Fareed. *In Defence of a Liberal Education* (W. W. Norton, 2015).

Zamora, Lois Parkinson, and Wendy B. Faris (eds.). *Magical Realism: Theory, History, Community* (Duke University Press, 1995).

Zuckerman, Ezra W. 'Typecasting and Generalism in Firm and Market: Genre-based Career Concentration in the Feature Film Industry, 1922-1995', *Transformation in Cultural Studies*, eds. Candace Jones and Patricia Thornton, *Research in the Sociology of Organizations* 23 (Elsevier, 2005).

ABOUT THE AUTHORS

KENNETH MIKKELSEN is a social philosopher. He helps people and organisations re-invent themselves to meet the challenges of tomorrow. Kenneth's work as a writer, speaker, leadership adviser and educator is centred around how we can live informed, meaningful lives and make wise choices that strengthen our society and leave a positive legacy for future generations. More details at kennethmikkelsen.com. Kenneth can be found on Twitter as @KenHMikkelsen.

RICHARD MARTIN is a freelance writer. In addition to co-authoring *The Neo-Generalist*, he is the author of the film noir study *Mean Streets and Raging Bulls*, as well as the ghostwriter of two books about leadership. Richard also provides editorial and advisory services, helping other authors bring their writing ideas to fruition. More details at richardmartinwriter.com.